the
PSYCHEDELIC
EXPERIENCE

the
PSYCHEDELIC EXPERIENCE

A Manual Based on the *Tibetan Book of the Dead*

Timothy Leary, Ph.D.
Ralph Metzner, Ph.D.
Richard Alpert, Ph.D.

CITADEL PRESS
Kensington Publishing Corp.
www.kensingtonbooks.com

CITADEL PRESS BOOKS are published by

Kensington Publishing Corp.
850 Third Avenue
New York, NY 10022

Originally published by Citadel in 1992, a new introduction by Daniel Pinchbeck has been added to this edition, and the book has been entirely reset, but it is otherwise unchanged.

The edition the Tibetan Book of the Dead used in this adaptation was published by Oxford University Press as *The Tibetan Book of the Dead, or The After-Death Experiences on the Bardo Plane,* according to Lama Kazi Dawa Samdup's English rendering, compiled and edited by W. Y. Evans-Wentz. Grateful acknowledgment is made to Mr. Evans-Wentz for the use of his material, hereinafter referred to as "Evans-Wentz."

All Kensington titles, imprints, and distributed lines are available at special quantity discounts for bulk purchases for sales promotions, premiums, fund-raising, educational, or institutional use. Special book excerpts or customized printings can also be created to fit specific needs. For details, write or phone the office of the Kensington special sales manager: Kensington Publishing Corp., 850 Third Avenue, New York, NY 10022, attn: Special Sales Department; phone 1-800-221-2647.

CITADEL PRESS and the Citadel logo are Reg. U.S. Pat. & TM Off.

First printing (with new introduction): November 2007

10 9 8 7

Printed in the United States of America

Library of Congress Control Number: 64019705

ISBN-13: 978-0-8065-1652-3
ISBN-10: 0-8065-1652-6

This version of the *Tibetan Book of the Dead*
is dedicated to

ALDOUS HUXLEY

July 26, 1894 – November 22, 1963
with profound admiration and gratitude.

"If you started in the wrong way," I said in answer to the investigator's questions, "everything that happened would be a proof of the conspiracy against you. It would all be self-validating. You couldn't draw a breath without knowing it was part of the plot."

"So you think you know where madness lies?"

My answer was a convinced and heartfelt, "Yes."

"And you couldn't control it?"

"No I couldn't control it. If one began with fear and hate as the major premise, one would have to go on to the conclusion."

"Would you be able," my wife asked, "to fix your attention on what the *Tibetan Book of the Dead* calls the Clear Light?"

I was doubtful.

"Would it keep the evil away, if you could hold it? Or would you not be able to hold it?"

I considered the question for some time. "Perhaps," I answered at last, "perhaps I could—but only if there were somebody there to tell me about the Clear Light. One couldn't do it by oneself. That's the point, I suppose, of the Tibetan ritual—somebody sitting there all the time and telling you what's what."

(*Doors of Perception,* 57–58)

Contents

Contents

Introduction (2007)

DANIEL PINCHBECK

IT HAS BEEN forty years since the heyday of the 1960s and the brief flowering of the psychedelic era that ended abruptly when Woodstock gave way to Altamont, the achievements of SDS (Students for a Democratic Society) were obscured by the terrorist acts of the Weathermen, and sensitive Beatles lyrics inspired the homicidal rages of Charles Manson's Family. Nobody can say for certain to what extent psychedelic use led to the radical inquiry and eventual degeneration of the 1960s spirit—it was certainly one element in a much larger story. In the wake of the '60s, many commentators from across the political spectrum found it convenient to blame psychedelics for some of the period's destructive excesses. Suppressed, interdicted, and generally reviled, mind-altering substances such as LSD, mescaline, mushrooms, and ayahuasca have not received a serious reconsideration since that time. Today, it is hard for us to imagine that long-ago moment when Ivy League professors, established intellectuals, film stars, famous poets, and millionaires sincerely believed that the exploration of non-ordinary states of consciousness through chemical means could induce a radical transformation of the individual and the society.

Within the broader context of this story, *The Psychedelic Experience: A Manual Based on the Tibetan Book of the Dead* is both a historical document and an anthropological curiosity. Written by a trio of renegade Harvard psychologists in 1962, *The Psychedelic Experience* was the first attempt to offer a written guide through the startling disjunctions, visionary vistas, disorienting droops into egolessness, and surges of ego inflation reliably induced by the ingestion of a sizable dose of a hallucinogen. The collaborators have attained legendary status in the intervening decades. Timothy Leary, charismatic ringmaster of the Harvard group, was soon to become the pied piper of the acid generation—using the mass media as a pulpit to proclaim his dicey message of "turn on, tune in, drop out"—before he fell into disgrace and disrepute. Richard Metzner went on to have a long career as a scholarly and meticulous advocate for the visionary experience, writing books such as *Ayahuasca: Human Consciousness and the Spirits of Nature* and *The Unfolding Self: Varieties of Transformative Experience*. Richard Alpert made the archetypal journey to India, where he found his guru, forsook LSD for yoga, and successfully rebranded himself. As Ram Dass, he has guided and inspired several generations of Western seekers.

By the time of the writing of *The Psychedelic Experience*, Leary, Metzner, and Alpert had abandoned the traditional methodologies of the social sciences for the intensive pursuit of mystical revelation and personal liberation. This change in focus happened in an extraordinarily compressed period of time. Leary's first psychedelic trip, on psilocybin, occurred in Mexico in 1960, as he approached his fortieth birthday. Returning to Harvard, he changed the subject of his research from interpersonal communication and what he termed "existential transactions" to an exploration of the possible uses of psychedelics for transforming personality and behavior. He launched a project in which prisoners were guided through psilocybin sessions to see if this would affect their rate of recidivism. At the same time, he gathered a circle of graduate students and like-minded professors around him in Cambridge, where they explored mushrooms and LSD together on a regular basis. The cultlike euphoria created by this investigation began to alienate the Harvard establishment. Ignoring the novelist Aldous Huxley's prudent warnings that "the only attitude for a researcher in this ticklish field is that of an anthropologist living in the midst of a tribe of potentially dangerous savages," Leary seemed to revel in defying convention and attracting attention to his antics. His increasingly erratic behavior led to reprimands and eventual dismissal. The Harvard coterie relocated to the Millbrook mansion in upstate New York, continuing their intellectual inquiry into the liberational potential of psychedelics—the scene was dubbed the "crypt trip" by Ken Kesey, who drove his magic bus of Merry Pranksters from the West Coast to Millbrook for a brief and famously uncomfortable summit.

The rediscovery of psychedelics in the late twentieth century caused shockwaves because the modern psyche had been cut off from the direct access to revelation formerly possessed by the shaman and seer.

Before the explosion of interest in the subject during the 1960s, direct visionary gnosis and shamanic techniques of ecstasy had been exiled and suppressed in the West for many hundreds of years. The witch hunts that took place during the Middle Ages launched a devastating assault on the last vestiges of indigenous shamanism and the orally transmitted knowledge and use of vision-inducing plants throughout Europe. During the era of Colonialism, Europeans sought to annihilate the traditional wisdom of those they conquered. Possessed by the hierarchical framework and transcendent ideology of Christianity, the Europeans crusaded against any and all representatives of the archaic worldview that knew second sight, visions, and prophecy to be crucial aspects of reality. With the rise of the modern scientific method, the only form of awareness that was seen as valid was empirical, rational, and materialist. Anything else was grist for romantic poetry or faint fever dreams.

As Harvard psychologists, Leary and his cohorts had high status and a role in maintaining the smooth functioning of the American machine. In the 1950s Cold War era, American psychology was biased toward naive behaviorism, prioritizing the objective and observable over the subjective and psychic. It is not surprising that the psychedelic trip, revealing multitudinous levels of awareness and secret domains of psychic activity, would have detonated within this mind-set with such tremendous, implosive force. "We're all schizophrenics now and we're in our own institution," Leary proclaimed in the wake of his first mushroom trip.

Wisdom, of course, is easier to obtain in hindsight. In hindsight, it is easy to see that it might have been prudent for Leary and his coterie to wait a number of years before proclaiming the psychedelic experience, in itself, as a fast track to "enlightenment," whatever that is. They might have restrained themselves, observing the longer-term effects of psychedelic use on themselves, their work, and their relationships. They might have seen the strategic value in maintaining their Ivy League connection and pedigree, even if it meant radically slowing down their experiments. Unfortunately, the psychologists had no background to prepare them for their sudden shift into expanded awareness—previously, their access to altered states had been through alcoholic inebriation, and the binge drinking endemic to 1950s professional life was as contractive as psychedelics were expansive. Their worldviews radically wrenched by a massive ingression of previously unknown psychic intensities, the Harvard psychologists grasped these chemical catalysts as the Answer, rather than approaching them, with skepticism and proper caution, as tools that, potentially containing hidden dangers, required scrupulous care.

The Psychedelic Experience is a cultural artifact of this early and pivotal time in the historical development of psychedelic use and understanding in the modern West. In their efforts to find a spiritual context for entheogenic exploration, the Harvard trio gravitated to the sacred culture of Tibetan Buddhism, interpreted in the groundbreaking works of W. Y. Evans-Wentz and Lama Govinda. In retrospect, this choice is interesting, on several levels. Although Leary had taken mushrooms for the first time in Mexico—he reported feeling that he understood the Mayan civilization for the first time during his trip—they did not create a manual based on indigenous practices or draw any connection to tribal shamanism in North or South America. Instead, they chose to contextualize the hallucinogenic journey in relation to the wisdom tradition of Tibet, which must have seemed far more distant in 1962 than it does today, when many Tibetan lamas have migrated to the United States, the Dalai Lama is a household name, and thousands pursue Tibetan Buddhist practices. Once again, a more cautious attitude might have mitigated the dangers of superficially appropriating the highly developed spiritual technology of a remote civilization. This quick grafting of entheogenic exploration onto Tibetan Buddhism could be seen as reflecting the absorptive ethos and narcissistic emphasis of our American mind-set, which tends to see all other cultures and resources as fodder to feed its experience, material desires, and knowledge base.

This manual may have helped to create a long-running rift in the spiritual culture of the modern-day West between followers of Buddhism and Yoga on one side and advocates of shamanic experimentation on the other. Although many Western Buddhists discovered the validity of expanded states of awareness through early psychedelic journeys, entheogenic use is frowned upon in traditional Buddhism and in modern adaptations of Eastern disciplines. The philosopher Ken Wilber draws a distinction between the experience of temporary "states" and the development of permanent "traits." While psychedelics can allow us to access different levels of awareness, their use does not necessarily compel a transformation that would turn the developmental possibilities glimpsed in those states—such as greater levels of empathy, a wider intellectual scope, a more refined aesthetic and sensuous engagement with the physical world, and so on—into positive character traits. Ego inflation and distorted judgment can be the result. A realistic reassessment of the use of psychedelic substances for personal development would reckon with both the positive and negative aspects of short- and long-term use, as well as the benefits of participating in shamanic work within an established tradition. We might find that psychedelic use can support a shift from "states" to "traits," but only within a larger framework and proper context for personal development.

Throughout *The Psychedelic Experience*, we find an emphasis, entirely lacking in the *Tibetan Book of the Dead*, on "the selfish, game-involved nature of man," "selfish game desire," "the return to game reality," "the ego-game," and so on. While Buddhism recognizes the "basic goodness" of our essential human nature, obscured by karma, the writers of the manual seem mired in a Puritanical and sin-stained conception of the individual. Apparently, the tripper's nefarious ambitions to succeed in the game-worlds of modern life needed to be purged in the hallucinatory fire of the entheogenic encounter. In this respect and many others, *The Psychedelic Experience* overlays a simplistic and moralizing psychological perspective on the subtler and more profound exegesis of an ancient spiritual science found in the original text.

As for the value of *The Psychedelic Experience* as a tripper's manual, it was certainty used for that purpose by thousands of people during the '60s, and may have provided a helpful reference point for some who would otherwise have plunged into their first journey with no context at all. In retrospect, however, the conjunction of bardo state experiences and psychedelic plateaux seems more than a bit forced, and the insistence on the desirability of losing the ego also seems naive. "Ego freedom" might be a more appropriate goal than "ego loss": the ego is our particular lens for perceiving reality, therefore loss of it would be devastating. However, if we could attain freedom from the ego, we could act out of a holistic awareness of our particular perspective in relation to larger social and evolutionary processes. John Lennon, who borrowed a few lines from the manual for a song ("Turn off your mind, relax, and float down stream . . ."), later told an interviewer, "I got a message on acid that you should destroy your ego, and I did, you know. I was reading that stupid book of Leary's and all that shit. We were going through a whole game that everyone went through, and I destroyed myself. . . . I destroyed my ego and I didn't believe I could do anything."

The psychedelic era of the 1960s could be seen as an attempted mass-cultural voyage of shamanic initiation. Because our culture lacked the proper frame of reference and background, as well as elders and wisdom-keepers who could guide the process, the effort reached a certain point and then short-circuited. Cultural figures like Leary and Lennon were thrust into the role of psychopomps, although they had not undergone the types of rigorous training demanded of shamanic candidates in traditional cultures. By the end of the 1960s, mechanisms of social repression—such as the Nixon-instituted "War on Drugs," which continues today, incarcerating millions of nonviolent users of interdicted substances—had kicked into gear. The movements of personal liberation made permanent changes in Western culture, but the initiatory process remained incomplete. Forty years after the "Summer of Love," it is possible that our culture is on the cusp of undergoing a second, much deeper phase of this initiatory journey.

As the pioneering psychedelic chemist Alexander Shulgin has pointed out, the idea that the Earth moved around the Sun was radical heresy at one time. A century later, it was a commonplace truism. The prospect that the inner exploration of consciousness with psychedelics might be recognized as, in itself, a positive and worthy endeavor is another radical heresy that may be seen as self-evident in the future. Rather than collapsing into anarchy, a civilization that supports the adult individual's right to utilize these chemical catalysts for self-discovery and spiritual communion might advance to a more mature and stable state. Much of the anxiety and negative conditioning around the subject could be dispelled with logical argument based on evidence for the relative safety of psychedelics, especially natural ones, compared to other drugs. The point is not that everyone needs to take psychedelics but that the minority of people who find themselves compelled to make this exploration could be permitted to do so.

There has been a huge evolution in our knowledge and use of psychedelics over the intervening decades. The growing curiosity and increasingly sophisticated knowledge base on the chemical and psychological mechanisms and spiritual value of psychedelics is supported by a cottage industry of books on the subject, ranging from the chemical recipes for mind-altering alkaloids presented in Alexander and Ann Shulgin's *PIKHAL* (*Phenethylamines I Have Known and Loved*) and *TIKHAL* (*Tryptamines . . .*) to Stanislav Grof's ground-breaking works on non-ordinary states of consciousness and the birth trauma, from Benny Shannon's *The Antipodes of the Mind: Charting the Phenomenology of the Ayahuasca Experience* to Andy Lechter's recent *Shroom: A Cultural History of the Magic Mushroom*, from anthropologist Jeremy Narby's *The Cosmic Serpent* to Dr. Rick Strassman's *DMT: The Spirit Molecule*, and many more. At the same time, various aspects of the psychedelic revelation that were so shocking to the generation coming of age in the 1960s have been seamlessly integrated into our new technologies, scientific paradigms, and pop culture.

In August, 2004, the English newspaper, *The Mail on Sunday*, reported that geneticist Frances Crick was taking low doses of LSD when he uncovered the double helix form of the DNA molecule in 1953 (Matt Ridley's 2006 biography, *Francis Crick, Discoverer of the Genetic Code*, also discusses Crick's LSD use). This bit of information, which Crick strenuously suppressed during his life, is only one of many examples of a secret "techgnostic" history linking psychedelic use with recent advances in human knowledge. The creation of the personal computer and the Internet was apparently fueled by crossover between techies and the psychedelic counterculture. This relationship is the subject of at least one recent book, *What the Doormouse Said*. The awareness of interconnectivity of consciousness often induced by psychedelics has been given visceral form through the continued development of the Net and "Web 2.0."

For the first time since the 1960s, the government and the academy are permitting scientific research into psychedelics, after a forty-year break. The Multidisciplinary Approach to Psychedelic Studies (MAPS) is one U.S. group that is currently shepherding a number of projects through the tangles of government bureaucracy. MAPS-sponsored studies currently under way examine the use of psilocybin to treat obsessive-compulsive disorders, the possible efficacy of MDMA to help terminally ill cancer patients prepare for death, and the use of the West African psychedelic iboga as a treatment for drug addiction. Unconnected to MAPS, a recent Johns Hopkins double-blind study essentially replicated experiments from the early 1960s, giving psilocybin and placebos to volunteers who had never experienced a psychedelic before. Sixty percent of the volunteers found their psilocybin sessions to be positive and in some cases spiritually transformative. While these results were unsurprising to anyone versed in psychedelic history, the study received surprisingly prominent media attention in the *Wall Street Journal*, on CNN, and elsewhere.

While scientific study of psychedelics picks up again, there is also an increasing openness toward the legally sanctioned use of natural "entheogens" (god-releasing chemicals) in established religious ritual. In 1993, Congress passed the emergency Religious Freedom Restoration Act, in reaction to a decision made by the U.S. Supreme Court that removed some federal protections from the Native American Church, which consumes the peyote cactus during all-night ceremonies. In 2005, following this new trend, the Court ruled in favor of Uniao do Vegetal, a Brazilian religion that uses the visionary potion ayahuasca as its sacrament. Ayahuasca contains the psychedelic dimethyltryptamine (DMT), which is endogenous to the human brain, and is found in many plants. Uniao do Vegetal is one of several authorized religions in Brazil that incorporate ayahuasca in their ceremonies and have official government approval as well as UN protection.

Outside of the scientific establishment and the religious context, personal experimentation with psychedelics remains popular in various subcultures across the United States. As the archives of the Vaults of Erowid (www.erowid.org) make abundantly clear, there are now many more people exploring a wider range of psychedelic compounds, from natural plants to recently discovered synthetic chemicals, than ever before. While the official interdiction continues in this country, we are in the throes of a global psychedelic renaissance that is, in many ways, far more extensive than that of the 1960s. Erowid features trip reports from individuals or small groups, sometimes taking substances in shamanic ritual, but often for purposes of inner exploration and hedonistic enjoyment.

It is possible that the current opening around this long-suppressed area of psychedelic vision foreshadows another bout of intense legal and social repression. However, it is also possible that a more profound, almost subliminal, shift is taking place, in attitudes toward the use of these substances, whether for personal exploration, shamanic vision, religious rite, or scientific study. In a culture that is awash in prescription chemicals, drugs of abuse, and mood-altering SSRIs, it seems increasingly odd to ban a handful of plant substances and related compounds (even LSD is closely related to a chemical found in ergot fungus) that have been used by human beings for untold thousands of years.

If psychedelics are making a resurgence at this time, this may be due to larger social forces. As in the 1960s, our civilization appears to have entered another phase of acute crisis—as well as, perhaps, evolutionary opportunity. To a large extent, the cultural and social movements of the 1960s developed in reaction to the Cold War, which nearly reached a devastating nuclear climax during the 1962 Cuban Missile Crisis. The awareness of humanity's hair-trigger proximity to self-inflicted annihilation inspired individual acts of courage and brilliance, and mass movements for social and personal liberation. It also led to widespread interest in psychedelic exploration as a fast track to self-knowledge and spiritual illumination. Rather than leading to instant "enlightenment," the visionary insights, temporary dissolution of ego boundaries, and deconditioning from proscribed social codes often induced by entheogenic explorations helped some people to reevaluate their own role in society at that time.

Today, we are faced with an intractable and unpopular war in Iraq that has already continued longer than the U.S. involvement in World War II, a rise in terrorism, and a global ecological crisis of terrifying magnitude. Just as the 1960s generation had to confront the militaristic insanity of the Vietnam War and the Cold War, our generation has to reckon with the individual and collective mind-set that has brought us to this critical threshold, quickly approaching the point of no return. While it would be the height of silliness to consider psychedelics, in themselves, as the Answer to the massive problems now facing us, they continue to offer some individuals a means for looking at the world from a different vantage point, integrating new levels of insight.

When we cast a cold eye on the current planetary situation, we discover that the industrial culture and excessive lifestyle of the affluent West masks an intensifying scarcity of resources that is unsustainable, even in the short term. According to scientists, 25 percent of all mammalian species will be extinct within the next thirty years. Our oceans are 90 percent fished out, with the potential for an irreversible collapse of many fisheries. As accelerating climate change leads to an increase in natural disasters, the polar ice caps are melting at rates that exceed predictions, potentially leading to a significant rise in global sea levels, causing coastal flooding. At current rates of deforestation, there will be no tropical forests left on the planet in forty years. According to many geologists, we are on the verge of "peak oil"—the highest *possible* production of oil, after which production must decline—leading to higher prices and potential scarcity of energy in the next decades. While thousands of new, barely tested chemicals and genetically engineered species are introduced to the global environment annually, the human sperm count is declining 1 percent per year—down 50 percent over the last half century, due to the spread of compounds such as pesticides and plastics that disrupt the endocrine system. Our efforts to find short-term technological fixes for the problems we create often lead to deeper errors and more dangerous unintended consequences. We are faced with the urgent task of changing the direction of global civilization if we want to avoid biospheric collapse and species burnout.

Without romanticizing native cultures, we can recognize that in many cases their intimate and sacralized relationship to the natural world kept them from overshooting the carrying capacities of their local ecosystems. The modern fixation on abstract, quantifiable, and rational modes of thought has profoundly alienated us from the directly sensorial and mimetic forms of knowing and relating maintained by indigenous cultures, allowing us to treat the natural world as something separate from ourselves. The entheogenic experience can temporarily reconnect the modern individual with lost participatory modes of awareness that may induce a greater sensitivity to his or her physical surroundings, beside raising a psychic periscope into the marginalized realms of mythological archetype and imaginative vision. It is not a question of forfeiting our modern cognition for fuzzy mysticism, but of reintegrating older and more intimate ways of knowing that can help us find a more balanced relationship with the human and nonhuman world around us.

It may seem unlikely that psychedelics could be rehabilitated, but who knows? Profound shifts in consciousness and culture happen in surprising ways, overturning the smug certitudes of academic experts and media commentators. New forms of awareness develop below everyday consciousness, gestating in hidden reaches of the collective psyche, long before they are allowed to be articulated and manifested as new social realities. What was once scandalous and impossible can become acceptable and obvious to a new generation, and doors that long seemed securely padlocked may swing open at the merest touch. As new paradigms of knowledge emerge, breaking through the crust of old habit and received conditioning, change becomes possible—and sometimes inevitable.

DANIEL PINCHBECK is the author of *Breaking Open the Head: A Psychedelic Journey into the Heart of Contemporary Shamanism* (Broadway Books, 2002) and *2012: The Return of Quetzalcoatl* (Tarcher/ Penguin, 2006). His writing has appeared in *The New York Times Magazine, Rolling Stone, ArtForum*, and many other publications. He is currently the editorial director of *Reality Sandwich* (realitysandwich. com), and a regular columnist for *Conscious Choice Magazine* (consciouschoice.com). In much of his recent work, he explores the profound implications of the shamanic experience and the possibility that a revival of archaic knowledge of visionary plants and psychedelic substances could accelerate a transformation of global consciousness.

I.
GENERAL
INTRODUCTION

A psychedelic experience is a journey to new realms of consciousness. The scope and content of the experience is limitless, but its characteristic features are the transcendence of verbal concepts, of space-time dimensions, and of the ego or identity. Such experiences of enlarged consciousness can occur in a variety of ways: sensory deprivation, yoga exercises, disciplined meditation, religious or aesthetic ecstasies, or spontaneously. Most recently they have become available to anyone through the ingestion of psychedelic drugs such as LSD, psilocybin, mescaline, DMT, etc.*

Of course, the drug does not produce the transcendent experience. It merely acts as a chemical key—it opens the mind, frees the nervous system of its ordinary patterns and structures. The nature of the experience depends almost entirely on set and setting. Set denotes the preparation of the individual, including his personality structure and his mood at the time. Setting is physical—the weather, the room's atmosphere; social—feelings of persons present towards one another; and cultural—prevailing views as to what is real. It is for this reason that manuals or guide-books are necessary. Their purpose is to enable a person to understand the new realities of the expanded consciousness, to serve as road maps for new interior territories which modern science has made accessible.

Different explorers draw different maps. Other manuals are to be written based on different models—scientific, aesthetic, therapeutic. The Tibetan model, on which this manual is based, is designed to teach the person to direct and control awareness in such a way as to reach that level of understanding variously called liberation, illumination, or enlightenment. If the manual is read several times before a session is attempted, and if a trusted person is there to remind and refresh the memory of the voyager during the experience, the consciousness will be freed from the games which comprise "personality" and from positive-negative hallucinations which often accompany states of ex-

---

*This is the statement of an ideal, not an actual situation, in 1964. The psychedelic drugs are in the United States classified as "experimental" drugs. That is, they are not available on a prescription basis, but only to "qualified investigators." The Federal Food and Drug Administration has defined "qualified investigators" to mean psychiatrists working in a mental hospital setting, whose research is sponsored by either state or federal agencies.

panded awareness. The *Tibetan Book of the Dead* was called in its own language the *Bardo Thödol*, which means "Liberation by Hearing on the After-Death Plane." The book stresses over and over that the free consciousness has only to hear and remember the teachings in order to be liberated.

The *Tibetan Book of the Dead* is ostensibly a book describing the experiences to be expected at the moment of death, during an intermediate phase lasting forty-nine (seven times seven) days, and during rebirth into another bodily frame. This however is merely the exoteric framework which the Tibetan Buddhists used to cloak their mystical teachings. The language and symbolism of death rituals of Bonism, the traditional pre-Buddhist Tibetan religion, were skillfully blended with Buddhist conceptions. The esoteric meaning, as it has been interpreted in this manual, is that it is death and rebirth of the ego that is described, not of the body. Lama Govinda indicates this clearly in his introduction when he writes: "It is a book for the living as well as for the dying." The book's esoteric meaning is often concealed beneath many layers of symbolism. It was not intended for general reading. It was designed to be understood only by one who was to be initiated personally by a *guru* into the Buddhist mystical doctrines, into the premortem-death-rebirth experience. These doctrines have been kept a closely guarded secret for many centuries, for fear that naive or careless application would do harm. In translating such an esoteric text, therefore, there are two steps: one, the rendering of the original text into English; and two, the practical interpretation of the text for its uses. In publishing this practical interpretation for use in the psychedelic drug session, we are in a sense breaking with the tradition of secrecy and thus contravening the teachings of the *lama-gurus*.

However, this step is justified on the grounds that the manual will not be understood by anyone who has not had a consciousness-expanding experience and that there are signs that the *lamas* themselves, after their recent diaspora, wish to make their teachings available to a wider public.

Following the Tibetan model then, we distinguish three phases of the psychedelic experience. The first period *(Chikhai Bardo)* is that of complete transcendence—beyond words, beyond space-time, beyond self. There are no visions, no sense of self, no thoughts. There are only pure awareness and ecstatic freedom from all game (and biological) involvements.* The second lengthy period involves self, or external game reality *(Chönyid Bardo)*—in sharp exquisite clarity or in the form of hallucinations (karmic apparitions). The final period *(Sidpa Bardo)* involves the return to routine game reality and the self. For most persons the second (aesthetic or hallucinatory) stage is the longest. For the initiated the first stage of illumination lasts longer. For the unprepared, the heavy game players, those who anxiously cling to their egos, and for those who take the drug in a non-supportive setting, the struggle to regain reality begins early and usually lasts to the end of their session.

Words like these are static, whereas the psychedelic experience is fluid and ever-changing. Typically the subject's consciousness flicks in and out of these three levels with rapid oscillations. One purpose of this manual is to enable the person to regain the transcendence of the First Bardo and to avoid prolonged entrapments in hallucinatory or ego-dominated game patterns.

The Basic Trusts and Beliefs. You must be ready to accept the possibility that there is a limitless range of awarenesses for which we now have no words; that awareness can expand beyond the range of your ego, your self, your familiar identity, beyond everything you have learned, beyond your notions of space and time, beyond the differences which usually separate people from each other and from the world around them.

You must remember that throughout human history, millions have made this voyage. A few (whom we call mystics, saints or buddhas) have made this experience endure and have communicated it to their fellow men. You must remember, too, that the experience is safe (at the very worst, you will end up the same person who entered the experience), and that all of the dangers which you have feared are unnecessary productions of your mind. Whether you experience heaven or hell, remember that it is your mind which creates them. Avoid grasping the

---

*"Games" are behavioral sequences defined by roles, rules, rituals, goals, strategies, values, language, characteristic space-time locations and characteristic patterns of movement. Any behavior not having these nine features is non-game: this includes physiological reflexes, spontaneous play, and transcendent awareness.

one or fleeing the other. Avoid imposing the ego game on the experience.

You must try to maintain faith and trust in the potentiality of your own brain and the billion-year-old life process. With your ego left behind you, the brain can't go wrong.

Try to keep the memory of a trusted friend or a respected person whose name can serve as guide and protection.

Trust your divinity, trust your brain, trust your companions.

Whenever in doubt, turn off your mind, relax, float downstream.

After reading this guide, the prepared person should be able, at the very beginning of his experience, to move directly to a state of non-game ecstasy and deep revelation. But if you are not well prepared, or if there is game distraction around you, you will find yourself dropping back. If this happens, then the instructions in Part IV should help you regain and maintain liberation. (pp. 95ff)

> Liberation in this context does not necessarily imply (especially in the case of the average person) the Liberation of Nirvana, but chiefly a liberation of the "life-flux" from the ego, in such manner as will afford the greatest possible consciousness and consequent happy rebirth. Yet for the very experienced and very highly efficient person, the [same] esoteric process of Transference* can be, according to the *lama-gurus*, so employed as to prevent any break in the flow of the stream of consciousness, from the moment of the ego-loss to the moment of a conscious rebirth (eight hours later). Judging from the translation made by the late Lama Kazi Dawa-Samdup, of an old Tibetan manuscript containing practical directions for ego-loss states, the ability to maintain a non-game ecstasy throughout the entire experience is possessed only by persons trained in mental concentration, or one-pointedness of mind, to such a high degree of proficiency as to be able to control all the mental functions and to shut out the distractions of the outside world. (Evans-Wentz, p. 86, note 2)

This manual is divided into four parts. The first part is introductory. The second is a step-by-step description of a psychedelic experience based directly on the Tibetan Book of the Dead. The third part contains

---

*Readers interested in a more detailed discussion of the process of "Transference" are referred to *Tibetan Yoga and Secret Doctrines*, edited by W. Y. Evans-Wentz, Oxford University Press, 1958.

practical suggestions on how to prepare for and conduct a psychedelic session. The fourth part contains instructive passages adapted from the *Bardo Thödol*, which may be read to the voyager during the session, to facilitate the movement of consciousness.

In the remainder of this introductory section, we review three commentaries on the Tibetan Book of the Dead, published with the Evans-Wentz edition. These are the introduction by Evans-Wentz himself, the distinguished translator-editor of four treatises on Tibetan mysticism; the commentary by Carl Jung, the Swiss psychoanalyst; and by Lama Govinda, an initiate of one of the principal Buddhist orders of Tibet.

A Tribute to W. Y. Evans-Wentz

Dr. Evans-Wentz, who literally sat at the feet of a Tibetan *lama* for years, in order to acquire his wisdom ... not only displays a deeply sympathetic interest in those esoteric doctrines so characteristic of the genius of the East, but likewise possesses the rare faculty of making them more or less intelligible to the layman.*

W. Y. Evans-Wentz is a great scholar who devoted his mature years to the role of bridge and shuttle between Tibet and the west: like an RNA molecule activating the latter with the coded message of the former. No greater tribute could be paid to the work of this academic liberator than to base our psychedelic manual upon his insights and to quote directly his comments on "the message of this book."

The message is, that the Art of Dying is quite as important as the Art of Living (or of Coming into Birth), of which it is the complement and summation; that the future of being is dependent, perhaps entirely, upon a rightly controlled death, as the second part of this volume, setting forth the Art of Reincarnating, emphasizes.

The Art of Dying, as indicated by the death-rite associated with initiation into the Mysteries of Antiquity, and referred to by Apuleius, the Platonic philosopher, himself an initiate, and by many other illustrious initiates, and as *The Egyptian Book of the Dead* suggests, appears to have been far better known to the ancient peoples inhabiting the Mediterranean countries than it is now by their descendants in Europe and the Americas.

To those who had passed through the secret experiencing of premortem death, right dying is initiation, conferring, as does the initiatory death-rite, the power to control consciously the process of death and regeneration. (Evans-Wentz, p. xiii-xiv)

The Oxford scholar, like his great predecessor of the eleventh century, Marpa ("The Translator"), who rendered Indian Buddhist texts into Tibetan, thereby preserving them from extinction, saw the vital importance of these doctrines and made them accessible to many. The "secret" is no longer hidden: "the art of dying is quite as important as the art of living."

*Quoted from a book review in *Anthropology* on the back of the Oxford University Press edition of the *Tibetan Book of the Dead*.

A Tribute to Carl G. Jung

Psychology is the systematic attempt to describe and explain man's behavior, both conscious and non-conscious. The scope of study is broad—covering the infinite variety of human activity and experience; and it is long—tracing back through the history of the individual, through the history of his ancestors, back through the evolutionary vicissitudes and triumphs which have determined the current status of the species. Most difficult of all, the scope of psychology is complex, dealing as it does with processes which are ever-changing.

Little wonder that psychologists, in the face of such complexity, escape into specialization and parochial narrowness.

A psychology is based on the available data and the psychologists' ability and willingness to utilize them. The behaviorism and experimentalism of twentieth-century western psychology is so narrow as to be mostly trivial. Consciousness is eliminated from the field of inquiry. Social application and social meaning are largely neglected. A curious ritualism is enacted by a priesthood rapidly growing in power and numbers.

Eastern psychology, by contrast, offers us a long history of detailed observation and systematization of the range of human consciousness along with an enormous literature of practical methods for controlling and changing consciousness. Western intellectuals tend to dismiss Oriental psychology. The theories of consciousness are seen as occult and mystical. The methods of investigating consciousness change, such as meditation, yoga, monastic retreat, and sensory deprivation, and are seen as alien to scientific investigation. And most damning of all in the eyes of the European scholar, is the alleged disregard of eastern psychologies for the practical, behavioral and social aspects of life. Such criticism betrays limited concepts and the inability to deal with the available historical data on a meaningful level. The psychologies of the east have always found practical application in the running of the state, in the running of daily life and family. A wealth of guides and handbooks exists: the *Book of Tao*, the *Analects of Confucius*, the *Gita*, the *I Ching,* the *Tibetan Book of the Dead*, to mention only the best-known.

Eastern psychology can be judged in terms of the use of available evidence. The scholars and observers of China, Tibet, and India went as far as their data allowed them. They lacked the findings of modern science and so their metaphors seem vague and poetic. Yet this does not negate their value. Indeed, eastern philosophic theories dating back four thousand years adapt readily to the most recent discoveries of nuclear physics, biochemistry, genetics, and astronomy.

A major task of any present day psychology—eastern or western—is to construct a frame of reference large enough to incorporate the recent findings of the energy sciences into a revised picture of man.

Judged against the criterion of the use of available fact, the greatest psychologists of our century are William James and Carl Jung.* Both of these men avoided the narrow paths of behaviorism and experimentalism. Both fought to preserve experience and consciousness as an area of scientific research. Both kept open to the advance of scientific theory and both refused to shut off eastern scholarship from consideration.

Jung used for his source of data that most fertile source—the internal. He recognized the rich meaning of the eastern message; he reacted to that great Rorschach inkblot, the *Tao Te Ching*. He wrote perceptive brilliant forewords to the *I Ching*, to the *Secret of the Golden Flower*, and struggled with the meaning of the *Tibetan Book of the Dead*. "For years, ever since it was first published, the *Bardo Thödol* has been my constant companion, and to it I owe not only many stimulating ideas and discoveries, but also many fundamental insights . . . Its philosophy contains the quintessence of Buddhist psychological criticism; and, as such, one can truly say that it is of an unexampled superiority."

> The *Bardo Thödol* is in the highest degree psychological in its outlook; but, with us, philosophy and theology are still in the mediaeval,

*To properly compare Jung with Sigmund Freud we must look at the available data which each man appropriated for his explorations. For Freud it was Darwin, classical thermodynamics, the Old Testament, Renaissance cultural history, and most important, the close overheated atmosphere of the Jewish family. The broader scope of Jung's reference materials assures that his theories will find a greater congeniality with recent developments in the energy sciences and the evolutionary sciences.

pre-psychological stage where only the assertions are listened to, explained, defended, criticized and disputed, while the authority that makes them has, by general consent, been deposed as outside the scope of discussion.

Metaphysical assertions, however, are *statements of the psyche*, and are therefore psychological. To the Western mind, which compensates its well-known feelings of resentment by a slavish regard for "rational" explanations, this obvious truth seems all too obvious, or else it is seen as an inadmissable negation of metaphysical "truth." Whenever the Westerner hears the word "psychological," it always sounds to him like "*only* psychological."

Jung draws upon Oriental conceptions of consciousness to broaden the concept of "projection":

Not only the "wrathful" but also the "peaceful" deities are conceived as *sangsāric* projections of the human psyche, an idea that seems all too obvious to the enlighted European, because it reminds him of his own banal simplifications. But though the European can easily explain away these deities as projections, he would be quite incapable of positing them at the same time as real. The *Bardo Thödol* can do that, because, in certain of its most essential metaphysical premises, it has the enlightened as well as the unenlightened European at a disadvantage. The ever-present, unspoken assumption of the *Bardo Thödol* is the anti-nominal character of all metaphysical assertions, and also the idea of the qualitative difference of the various levels of consciousness and of the metaphysical realities conditioned by them. The background of this unusual book is not the niggardly European "either-or," but a magnificently affirmative "both-and." This statement may appear objectionable to the Western philosopher, for the West loves clarity and unambiguity; consequently, one philosopher clings to the position, "God is," while another clings equally fervently to the negation, "God is not."

Jung clearly sees the power and breadth of the Tibetan model but occasionally he fails to grasp its meaning and application. Jung, too, was limited (as we all are) to the social models of his tribe. He was a psychoanalyst, the father of a school. Psychotherapy and psychiatric diagnosis were the two applications which came most naturally to him.

Jung misses the central concept of the Tibetan book. This is not (as Lama Govinda reminds us) a book of the dead. It is a book of the dying; which is to say a book of the living; it is a book of life and how to live. The concept of actual physical death was an exoteric facade adopted to fit the prejudices of the Bonist tradition in Tibet. Far from being an embalmers' guide, the manual is a detailed account of how to lose the ego; how to break out of personality into new realms of consciousness; and how to avoid the involuntary limiting processes of the ego; how to make the consciousness-expansion experience endure in subsequent daily life.

Jung struggles with this point. He comes close but never quite clinches it. He had nothing in his conceptual framework which could make practical sense out of the ego-loss experience.

> The *Tibetan Book of the Dead*, or the *Bardo Thödol*, is a book of instructions for the dead and dying. Like *The Egyptian Book of the Dead* it is meant to be a guide for the dead man during the period of his *Bardo* existence.

In this quote Jung settles for the exoteric and misses the esoteric. In a later quote he seems to come closer:

> The instruction given in the *Bardo Thödol* serves to recall to the dead man the experiences of his initiation and the teachings of his *guru*, for the instruction is, at bottom, nothing less than an initiation of the dead into the Bardo life, just as the initiation of the living was a preparation for the Beyond. Such was the case, at least, with all the mystery cults in ancient civilizations from the time of the Egyptian and Eleusinian mysteries. In the initiation of the living, however, this "Beyond" is not a world beyond death, but a reversal of the mind's intentions and outlook, a psychological "Beyond" or, in Christian terms, a "redemption" from the trammels of the world and of sin. Redemption is a separation and deliverance from an earlier condition of darkness and unconsciousness, and leads to a condition of illumination and releasedness, to victory and transcendence over everything "given."
>
> Thus far the *Bardo Thödol* is, as Dr. Evans-Wentz also feels, an initiation process whose purpose it is to restore to the soul the divinity it lost at birth.

In still another passage Jung continues the struggle but misses again:

> Nor is the psychological use we make of it (the Tibetan Book) anything but a secondary intention, though one that is possibly sanc-

tioned by *lamaist* custom. The real purpose of this singular book is the attempt, which must seem very strange to the educated European of the twentieth century, to enlighten the dead on their journey through the regions of the *Bardo*. The Catholic Church is the only place in the world of the white man where any provision is made for the souls of the departed.

In the summary of Lama Govinda's comments which follow we shall see that the Tibetan commentator, freed from the European concepts of Jung, moves directly to the esoteric and practical meaning of the Tibetan book.

In his autobiography (written in 1960) Jung commits himself wholly to the inner vision and to the wisdom and superior reality of internal perceptions. In 1938 (when his Tibetan commentary was written) he was moving in this direction but cautiously and with the ambivalent reservations of the psychiatrist *cum* mystic.

The dead man must desperately resist the dictates of reason, as we understand it, and give up the supremacy of egohood, regarded by reason as sacrosanct. What this means in practice is complete capitulation to the objective powers of the psyche, with all that this entails; a kind of symbolical death, corresponding to the Judgement of the Dead in the *Sidpa Bardo*. It means the end of all conscious, rational, morally responsible conduct of life, and a voluntary surrender to what the *Bardo Thödol* calls "*karmic* illusion." *Karmic* illusion springs from belief in a visionary world of an extremely irrational nature, which neither accords with nor derives from our rational judgments but is the exclusive product of uninhibited imagination. It is sheer dream or "fantasy," and every well-meaning person will instantly caution us against it; nor indeed can one see at first sight what is the difference between fantasies of this kind and the phantasmagoria of a lunatic. Very often only a slight *abaissement du niveau mental* is needed to unleash this world of illusion. The terror and darkness of this moment has its equivalent in the experiences described in the opening sections of the *Sidpa Bardo*. But the contents of this *Bardo* also reveal the archetypes, the *karmic* images which appear first in their terrifying form. The *Chönyid* state is equivalent to a deliberately induced psychosis. . . .

The transition, then, from the *Sidpa* state to the *Chönyid* state is a dangerous reversal of the aims and intentions of the conscious mind. It is a sacrifice of the ego's stability and a surrender to the extreme uncertainty of what must seem like a chaotic riot of phantasmal forms. When Freud coined the phrase that the ego was "the true seat of anxiety," he was giving voice to a very true and profound intuition. Fear of self-sacrifice lurks deep in every ego, and this fear is often only the precariously controlled demand of the unconscious forces to burst out in full strength. No one who strives for selfhood (individuation) is spared this dangerous passage, for that which is feared also belongs to the wholeness of the self—the sub-human, or supra-human, world of psychic "dominants" from which the ego originally emancipated itself with enormous effort, and then only partially, for the sake of a more or less illusory freedom. This liberation is certainly a very necessary and very heroic undertaking, but it represents nothing final: it is merely the creation of a *subject*, who, in order to find fulfillment, has still to be confronted by an *object*. This, at first sight, would appear to be the world, which is swelled out with projections for that very purpose. Here we seek and find our difficulties, here we seek and find our enemy, here we seek and find what is dear and precious to us; and it is comforting to know that all evil and all good is to be found out there, in the visible object, where it can be conquered, punished, destroyed or enjoyed. But nature herself does not allow this paradisal state of innocence to continue for ever. There are, and always have been, those who cannot help but see that the world and its experiences are in the nature of a symbol, and that it really reflects something that lies hidden in the subject himself, in his own transubjective reality. It is from this profound intuition, according to *lamaist* doctrine, that the *Chönyid* state derives its true meaning, which is why the *Chönyid Bardo* is entitled "The *Bardo* of the Experiencing of Reality."

The reality experienced in the *Chönyid* state is, as the last section of the corresponding *Bardo* teaches, the reality of thought. The "thought-forms" appear as realities, fantasy takes on real form, and the terrifying dream evoked by *karma* and played out by the unconscious "dominants" begins.

Jung would not have been surprised by professional and institutional antagonism to psychedelics. He closes his Tibetan commentary with a poignant political aside:

The *Bardo Thödol* began by being a "closed" book, and so it has remained, no matter what kind of commentaries may be written upon it. For it is a book that will only open itself to spiritual understanding and this is a capacity which no man is born with, but which he can only acquire through special training and special experience. It is good that such to all intents and purposes "useless" books exist. They are meant for those "queer folk" who no longer set much store by the uses, aims, and meaning of present-day "civilization."

To provide "special training" for the "special experience" provided by psychedelic materials is the purpose of this version of the *Tibetan Book of the Dead.*

A Tribute to Lama Anagarika Govinda

In the preceding section the point was made that eastern philosophy and psychology—poetic, indeterministic, experiential, inward-looking, vaguely evolutionary, open-ended—is more easily adapted to the findings of modern science than the syllogistic, certain, experimental, externalizing logic of western psychology. The latter imitates the irrelevant rituals of the energy sciences but ignores the data of physics and genetics, the meanings and implications.

Even Carl Jung, the most penetrating of the western psychologists, failed to understand the basic philosophy of the *Bardo Thödol*.

Quite in contrast are the comments on the Tibetan manual by Lama Anagarika Govinda.

His opening statement at first glance would cause a Judaeo-Christian psychologist to snort in impatience. But a close look at these phrases reveals that they are the poetic statement of the genetic situation as currently described by biochemists and DNA researchers.

> It may be argued that nobody can talk about death with authority who has not died; and since nobody, apparently, has ever returned from death, how can anybody know what death is, or what happens after it?
>
> The Tibetan will answer: "There is not *one* person, indeed, not *one* living being, that has *not* returned from death. In fact, we all have died many deaths, before we came into this incarnation. And what we call birth is merely the reverse side of death, like one of the two sides of a coin, or like a door which we call "entrance" from outside and "exit" from inside a room.

The *lama* then goes on to make a second poetic comment about the potentialities of the nervous system, the complexity of the human cortical computer.

> It is much more astonishing that not everybody remembers his or her previous death; and, because of this lack of remembering, most persons do not believe there was a previous death. But, likewise, they do not remember their recent birth—and yet they do not doubt that they were recently born. They forget that active memory is only a small part of our normal consciousness, and that our subconscious memory registers and preserves every past impression and experience which our waking mind fails to recall.

The *lama* then proceeds to slice directly to the esoteric meaning of the *Bardo Thödol*—that core meaning which Jung and indeed most European Orientalists have failed to grasp.

> For this reason, the *Bardo Thödol*, the Tibetan book vouchsafing liberation from the intermediate state between life and re-birth,—which state men call death,—has been couched in symbolical language. It is a book which is sealed with the seven seals of silence,—not because its knowledge should be withheld from the uninitiated, but because its knowledge would be misunderstood, and, therefore, would tend to mislead and harm those who are unfitted to receive it. But the time has come to break the seals of silence; for the human race has come to the juncture where it must decide whether to be content with the subjugation of the material world, or to strive after the conquest of the spiritual world, by subjugating selfish desires and transcending self-imposed limitations.

The *lama* next describes the effects of consciousness-expansion techniques. He is talking here about the method he knows—the Yogic—but his words are equally applicable to psychedelic experience.

> There are those who, in virtue of concentration and other *yogic* practices, are able to bring the subconscious into the realm of discriminative consciousness and, thereby, to draw upon the unrestricted treasury of subconscious memory, wherein are stored the records not only of our past lives but the records of the past of our race, the past of humanity, and of all pre-human forms of life, if not of the very consciousness that makes life possible in this universe.
>
> If, through some trick of nature, the gates of an individual's subconsciousness were suddenly to spring open, the unprepared mind would be overwhelmed and crushed. Therefore, the gates of the subconscious are guarded, by all initiates, and hidden behind the veil of mysteries and symbols.

In a later section of his foreword the *lama* present a more detailed elaboration of the inner meaning of the *Thödol*.

> If the *Bardo Thödol* were to be regarded as being based merely upon folklore, or as consisting of religious speculation about death and a hypothetical after-death state, it would be of interest only to anthropologists and students of religion. But the *Bardo Thödol* is far more. It is a key to the innermost recesses of the human mind, and a guide for initiates, and for those who are seeking the spiritual path of liberation.

Although the *Bardo Thödol* is at present time widely used in Tibet as a breviary, and read or recited on the occasion of death,—for which reason it has been aptly called "The Tibetan Book of the Dead"—one should not forget that it was originally conceived to serve as a guide not only for the dying and the dead, but for the living as well. And herein lies the justification for having made the *Tibetan Book of the Dead* accessible to a wider public.

Notwithstanding the popular customs and beliefs which, under the influence of age-old traditions of pre-Buddhist origin, have grown around the profound revelations of the *Bardo Thödol*, it has value only for those who practise and realize its teaching during their lifetime.

There are two things which have caused misunderstanding. One is that the teachings seem to be addressed to the dead or the dying; the other that the title contains the expression "Liberation through Hearing" (in Tibetan, *Thos-grol*). As a result, there has arisen the belief that it is sufficient to read or to recite the *Bardo Thödol* in the presence of a dying person, or even of a person who has just died, in order to effect his or her liberation.

Such misunderstanding could only have arisen among those who do not know that it is one of the oldest and most universal practices for the initiate to go through the experience of death before he can be spiritually reborn. Symbolically he must die to his past, and to his old ego, before he can take his place in the new spiritual life into which he has been initiated.

The dead or the dying person is addressed in the *Bardo Thödol* mainly for three reasons: (1) the earnest practitioner of these teachings should regard every moment of his or her life as if it were the last; (2) when a follower of these teachings is actually dying, he or she should be reminded of the experiences at the time of initiation, or of the words (or *mantra*) of the *guru*, especially if the dying one's mind lacks alertness during the critical moments; and (3) one who is still incarnate should try to surround the person dying, or just dead, with loving and helpful thoughts during the first stages of the new, or afterdeath, state of existence, without allowing emotional attachment to interfere or to give rise to a state of morbid mental depression. Accordingly, one function of the *Bardo Thödol* appears to be more to help those who have been left behind to adopt the right attitude towards the dead and towards the fact of death than to assist the dead, who, according to Buddhist belief, will not deviate from their own *karmic* path. . . .

This proves that we have to do here with life itself and not merely with a mass for the dead, to which the *Bardo Thödol* was reduced in later times. . . .

Under the guise of a science of death, the *Bardo Thödol* reveals the secret of life; and therein lies its spiritual value and its universal appeal.

Here then is the key to a mystery which has been passed down for over 2,500 years—the consciousness-expansion experience—the pre-mortem death and rebirth rite. The Vedic sages knew the secret; the Eleusinian initiates knew it; the Tantrics knew it. In all their esoteric writings they whisper the message: it is possible to cut beyond ego-consciousness, to tune in on neurological processes which flash by at the speed of light, and to become aware of the enormous treasury of ancient racial knowledge welded into the nucleus of every cell in your body.

Modern psychedelic chemicals provide a key to this forgotten realm of awareness. But just as this manual without the psychedelic awareness is nothing but an exercise in academic Tibetology, so, too, the potent chemical key is of little value without the guidance and the teachings.

Westerners do not accept the existence of conscious processes for which they have no operational term. The attitude which is prevalent is:—if you can't label it, and if it is beyond current notions of space-time and personality, then it is not open for investigation. Thus we see the ego-loss experience confused with schizophrenia. Thus we see present-day psychiatrists solemnly pronouncing the psychedelic keys as psychosis-producing and dangerous.

The new visionary chemicals and the pre-mortem-death-rebirth experience may be pushed once again into the shadows of history. Looking back, we remember that every middle-eastern and European administrator (with the exception of certain periods in Greece and Persia) has, during the last three thousand years, rushed to pass laws against any emerging transcendental process, the pre-mortem-death-rebirth session, its adepts, and any new method of consciousness-expansion.

The present moment in human history (as Lama Govinda points out) is critical. Now, for the first time, we possess the means of providing the enlightenment to any prepared volunteer. (The enlightenment always comes, we remember, in the form of a new energy process, a physical, neurological event.) For these reasons we have prepared this psychedelic version of the *Tibetan Book of the Dead*. The secret is released once again, in a new dialect, and we sit back quietly to observe whether man is ready to move ahead and to make use of the new tools provided by modern science.

II.
THE TIBETAN
BOOK OF
THE DEAD

First Bardo:
The Period of Ego-Loss
or Non-Game Ecstasy
(Chikhai Bardo)

Part I: The Primary Clear Light Seen at the Moment of Ego-Loss

All individuals who have received the practical teachings of this manual will, if the text be remembered, be set face to face with the ecstatic radiance and will win illumination instantaneously, without entering upon hallucinatory struggles and without further suffering on the age-long pathway of normal evolution which traverses the various worlds of game existence.

This doctrine underlies the whole of the Tibetan model. Faith is the first step on the "Secret Pathway." Then comes illumination and with it certainty; and when the goal is won, emancipation. Success implies very unusual preparation in consciousness expansion, as well as much calm, compassionate game playing (good *karma*) on the part of the participant. If the participant can be made to see and to grasp the idea of the empty mind as soon as the guide reveals it—that is to say, if he has the power to die consciously—and, at the supreme moment of quitting the ego, can recognize the ecstasy which will dawn upon him then, and become one with it, all game bonds of illusion are broken asunder immediately: the dreamer is awakened into reality simultaneously with the mighty achievement of recognition.

It is best if the *guru* (spiritual teacher), from whom the participant received guiding instructions, is present, but if the *guru* cannot be present, then another experienced person; or if the latter is also unavailable, then a person whom the participant trusts should be available to read this manual without imposing any of his own games. Thereby the participant will be put in mind of what he had previously heard of the experience and will at once come to recognize the fundamental Light and undoubtedly obtain liberation.

Liberation is the nervous system devoid of mental-conceptual activity.* The mind in its conditioned state, that is to say, when limited to words and ego games, is continuously in thought-formation activity. The nervous system in a state of quiescence, alert, awake but not active is comparable to what Buddhists call the highest state of *dhyāna* (deep meditation) when still united to a human body. The conscious recognition of the Clear Light induces an ecstatic condition of consciousness such as saints and mystics of the West have called illumination.

The first sign is the glimpsing of the "Clear Light of Reality," "the infallible mind of the pure mystic state." This is the awareness of energy transformations with no imposition of mental categories.

The duration of this state varies with the individual. It depends upon

---

*Realization of the Voidness, the Unbecome, the Unborn, the Unmade, the Unformed, implies Buddhahood, Perfect Enlightenment—the state of the divine mind of the Buddha. It may be helpful to remember that this ancient doctrine is not in conflict with modern physics. The theoretical physicist and cosmologist, George Gamow, presented in 1950 a viewpoint which is close to the phenomenological experience described by the Tibetan *lamas.*

> If we imagine history running back in time, we inevitably come to the epoch of the "big squeeze" with all the galaxies, stars, atoms and atomic nuclei squeezed, so to speak, to a pulp. During that early stage of evolution, matter must have been dissociated into its elementary components. . . . We call this primordial mixture ylem.

At this first point in the evolution of the present cycle, according to this first-rank physicist, there existed only the Unbecome, the Unborn, the Unformed. And this, according to astrophysicists, is the way it will end; the silent unity of the Unformed. The Tibetan Buddhists suggest that the uncluttered intellect can experience what astrophysics confirms. The Buddha *Vairochana*, the *Dhyānī Buddha* of the Center. Manifester of Phenomena, is the highest path to enlightenment. As the source of all organic life, in him all things visible and invisible have their consummation and absorption. He is associated with the Central Realm of the Densely-Packed, i.e., the seed of all universal forces and things are densely packed together. This remarkable convergence of modern astrophysics and ancient *lamaism* demands no complicated explanation. The cosmological awareness—and awareness of every other natural process—is there in the cortex. You can confirm this pre-conceptual mystical knowledge by empirical observation and measurement, but it's all there inside your skull. Your neurons "know" because they are linked directly to the process, are part of it.

experience, security, trust, preparation and the surroundings. In those who have had even a little practical experience of the tranquil state of non-game awareness, and in those who have happy games, this state can last from thirty minutes to several hours.

In this state, realization of what mystics call the "Ultimate Truth" is possible, provided that sufficient preparation has been made by the person beforehand. Otherwise he cannot benefit now, and must wander on into lower and lower conditions of hallucinations, as determined by his past games, until he drops back to routine reality.

It is important to remember that the consciousness-expansion process is the reverse of the birth process, birth being the beginning of game life and the ego-loss experience being a temporary ending of game life. But in both there is a passing from one state of consciousness into another. And just as an infant must wake up and learn from experience the nature of this world, so likewise a person at the moment of consciousness expansion must wake up in this new brilliant world and become familiar with its own peculiar conditions.

In those who are heavily dependent on their ego games, and who dread giving up their control, the illuminated state endures only so long as it would take to snap a finger. In some, it lasts as long as the time taken for eating a meal.

If the subject is prepared to diagnose the symptoms of ego loss, he needs no outside help at this point. Not only should the person about to give up his ego be able to diagnose the symptoms as they come, one by one, but he should also be able to recognize the Clear Light without being set face to face with it by another person. If the person fails to recognize and accept the onset of ego loss, he may complain of strange bodily symptoms. This shows that he has not reached a liberated state. Then the guide or friend should explain the symptoms as indicating the onset of ego loss.

Here is a list of commonly reported physical sensations:

1. Bodily pressure, which the Tibetans call earth-sinking-into-water;
2. Clammy coldness, followed by feverish heat, which the Tibetans call water-sinking-into-fire;

3. Body disintegrating or blown to atoms, called fire-sinking-into-air;
4. Pressure on head and ears, which Americans call rocket-launching-into-space;
5. Tingling in extremities;
6. Feelings of body melting or flowing as if wax;
7. Nausea;
8. Trembling or shaking, beginning in pelvic regions and spreading up torso.

These physical reactions should be recognized as signs heralding transcendence. Avoid treating them as symptoms of illness, accept them, merge with them, enjoy them.

Mild nausea occurs often with the ingestion of morning-glory seeds or peyote, rarely with mescaline and infrequently with LSD or psilocybin. If the subject experiences stomach messages, they should be hailed as a sign that consciousness is moving around in the body. The symptoms are mental; the mind controls the sensation, and the subject should merge with the sensation, experience it fully, enjoy it and, having enjoyed it, let consciousness flow on to the next phase. It is usually more natural to let consciousness stay in the body—the subject's attention can move from the stomach and concentrate on breathing, heart beat. If this does not free him from nausea, the guide should move the consciousness to external events—music, walking in the garden, etc.

The appearance of physical symptoms of ego-loss, recognized and understood, should result in peaceful attainment of illumination. If ecstatic acceptance does not occur (or when the period of peaceful silence seems to be ending), the relevant sections of the instructions (pp. 97ff) can be spoken in a low tone of voice in the ear. It is often useful to repeat them distinctly, clearly impressing them upon the person so as to prevent his mind from wandering. Another method of guiding the experience with a minimum of activity is to have the instructions previously recorded in the subject's own voice and to flip the tape on at the appropriate moment. The reading will recall to the mind of the voyager the former preparation; it will cause the naked consciousness to be recognized as the "Clear Light of the Beginning;" it

will remind the subject of his unity with this state of perfect enlightenment and help him maintain it.

If, when undergoing ego-loss, one is familiar with this state, by virtue
of previous experience and preparation, the Wheel of Rebirth (i.e., all
game playing) is stopped, and liberation instantaneously is achieved.
But such spiritual efficiency is so very rare, that the normal mental
condition of the person is unequal to the supreme feat of holding on to
the state in which the Clear Light shines; and there follows a progres-
sive descent into lower and lower states of the Bardo existence, and
then rebirth. The simile of a needle balanced and set rolling on a thread
is used by the *lamas* to elucidate this condition. So long as the needle
retains its balance, it remains on the thread. Eventually, however, the
law of gravitation (the pull of the ego or external stimulation) affects
it, and it falls. In the realm of the Clear Light, similarly, the mentality
of a person in the ego-transcendent state momentarily enjoys a condition of balance, of perfect equilibrium, and of oneness. Unfamiliar with
such a state, which is an ecstatic state of non-ego, the consciousness of
the average human being lacks the power to function in it. *Karmic* (i.e.,
game) propensities becloud the consciousness-principle with thoughts
of personality, of individualized being, of dualism. Thus, losing equilibrium, consciousness falls away from the Clear Light. It is thought
processes which prevent the realization of *Nirvāna* (which is the
"blowing out of the flame" of selfish game desire); and so the Wheel
of Life continues to turn.

All or some of the appropriate passages in the instructions (pp. 97ff)
may be read to the voyager during the period of waiting for the drug to
take effect, and when the first symptoms of ego-loss appear. When the
voyager is clearly in a profound ego-transcendent ecstasy, the wise
guide will remain silent.

Part II: The Secondary Clear Light Seen Immediately After Ego-Loss

The preceding section describes how the Clear Light may be recognized and liberation maintained. But if it becomes apparent that the Primary Clear Light has not been recognized, then it can certainly be assumed there is dawning what is called the phase of the Secondary Clear Light. The first flash of experience usually produces a state of ecstasy of the greatest intensity. Every cell in the body is sensed as involved in orgastic creativity.

It may be helpful to describe in more detail some of the phenomena which often accompany the moment of ego-loss. One of these might be called "wave energy flow." The individual becomes aware that he is part of and surrounded by a charged field of energy, which seems almost electrical. In order to maintain the ego-loss state as long as possible, the prepared person will relax and allow the forces to flow through him. There are two dangers to avoid: the attempt to control or to rationalize this energy flow. Either of these reactions is indicative of ego-activity and the First Bardo transcendence is lost.

The second phenomenon might be called "biological life-flow." Here the person becomes aware of physiological and biochemical processes; rhythmic pulsing activity within the body. Often this may be sensed as powerful motors or generators continuously throbbing and radiating energy. An endless flow of cellular forms and colors flashes by. Internal biological processes may also be heard with characteristic swooshing, crackling, and pounding noises. Again the person must resist the temptation to label or control these processes. At this point you are tuned in to areas of the nervous system which are inaccessible to routine perception. You cannot drag your ego into the molecular processes of life. These processes are a billion years older than the learned conceptual mind.

Another typical and most rewarding phase of the First Bardo involves ecstatic energy movement felt in the spine. The base of the backbone seems to be melting or seems on fire. If the person can maintain quiet concentration the energy will be sensed as flowing upwards. Tantric adepts devote decades of concentrated meditation to the release of these ecstatic energies which they call *Kundalini*, the Serpent Power. One allows the energies to travel upwards through several ganglionic centers *(chakras)* to the brain, where they are sensed as a burning sensation in the top of the cranium. These sensations are not unpleasant to the prepared person, but, on the contrary, are accompanied by the most intense feelings of joy and illumination. Ill-prepared subjects may interpret the experience in pathological terms and attempt to control it, usually with unpleasant results.*

If the subject fails to recognize the rushing flow of First Bardo phenomena, liberation from the ego is lost. The person finds himself slipping back into mental activities. At this point he should try to recall the instructions or be reminded of them, and a second contact with these processes can be made.

The second stage is less intense. A ball set bouncing reaches its greatest height at the first bounce; the second bounce is lower, and each succeeding bounce is still lower until the ball comes to rest. The consciousness at the loss of the ego is similar to this. Its first spiritual bound, directly upon leaving the body-ego, is the highest; the next is lower. Then the force of *karma*, (i.e., past game-playing), takes over and different forms of external reality are experienced. Finally, the force of *karma* having spent itself, consciousness returns to "normal." Routines are taken up again and thus rebirth occurs.

The first ecstasy usually ends with a momentary flashback to the ego condition. This return can be happy or sad, loving or suspicious, fearful or courageous, depending on the personality, the preparation, and the setting.

---

*Professor R. C. Zaehner, who as an Oriental scholar and "expert" on mysticism should have known better, has published an account of how this prized experience can be lost and distorted into hypochondriacal complaint in the ill-educated.

> . . . I had a curious sensation in my body which reminded me of what Mr. Custance describes as a "tingling at the base of the spine," which according to him, usually precedes a bout of mania. It was rather like that. In the Broad Walk this sensation occurred, but more strongly. It felt as if something warm were surging up my body. The sensation occurred again and again until the climax of the experiment was reached . . . I did not like it at all.

(R. C. Zaehner: *Mysticism, Sacred and Profane.* Oxford Univ. Press, 1957, p. 214)

This flashback to the ego-game is accompanied by a concern with identity. "Who am I now? Am I dead or not dead? What is happening?" You cannot determine. You see the surroundings and your companions as you had been used to seeing them before. There is a penetrating sensitivity. But you are on a different level. Your ego grasp is not quite as sure as it was.

The *karmic* hallucinations and visions have not yet started. Neither the frightening apparitions nor the heavenly visions have begun. This is a most sensitive and pregnant period. The remainder of the experience can be pushed one way or another depending upon preparation and emotional climate.

If you are experienced in consciousness alteration, or if you are a naturally introverted person, remember the situation and the schedule. Stay calm and let the experience take you where it will. You will probably re-experience the ecstasy of illumination once again; or you may drift into aesthetic or philosophic or interpersonal enlightenments. Don't hold on: let the stream carry you along.

The experienced person is usually beyond dependence on setting. He can turn off external pressure and return to illumination. An extroverted person, dependent upon social games and outside situations may, however, become pleasantly distracted (colors, sounds, people). If you anticipate extroverted distraction and if you want to maintain a non-game state of ecstasy, then remember the following suggestions: do not be distracted; try to concentrate on an ideal contemplative personage, e.g., Buddha, Christ, Socrates, Ramakrishna, Einstein, Herman Hesse or Lao Tse: follow his model as if he were a being with a physical body waiting for you. Join him.

If this is not successful, don't fret or think about it. Perhaps you don't have a mystical or transcendental ideal. That means your conceptual limits are within external games. Now that you know what the mystic experience is, you can prepare for it next time. You have lost the content-free flow and should now be ready to slip into exciting confrontation with external reality. In the Second Bardo you can reach and deeply experience game revelations.

We have just anticipated the reactions of the naturally mystical introvert, the experienced person, and the extrovert. Now let's turn to the novitiate who shows confusion at this early stage of the sequence. The best procedure is to make a reassuring sign and do nothing. He will have read this manual and will have some guidepost. Leave him alone and he will probably dive into his panic and master it. If he indicates that he wishes guidance, repeat the instructions. Tell him what is happening. Remind him of his phase in the process. Urge him quietly to release his ego struggle and drift back into contact with the Clear Light.

Preparation and guidance of this sort will allow many to reach the illuminated state who would not be expected to recognize it.

At this point, it is necessary to inject a word of benign warning. Reading this manual is extremely useful, but no words can communicate experience. You are going to be surprised, startled and delighted. A person may have heard a detailed description of the art of swimming and yet never had the chance to swim. Suddenly diving into the water, he finds himself unable to swim. So with those who have tried to learn the theory of how to experience ego-loss, and have never applied it. They cannot maintain unbroken continuity of consciousness, they grow bewildered at the changed condition; they fail to maintain the mystical ecstasy; they fail to take advantage of the opportunity unless upheld and directed by a guide. Even with all that a guide can do, they ordinarily, because of bad *karma* (heavy ego games) fail to recognize the liberation. But this is no cause for worry. At the worst, they just slip back to shore. No one has drowned, and most of those who have taken the voyage have been eager to try again.

Even those who have familiarized themselves with the road maps and who previously have had illumination, may find themselves in settings where heavy game behavior on the part of others forces them into contact with external reality. If this happens, recall the instructions. The person who masters this principle can block out the external. The one who has mastered control of consciousness is independent of setting.

Again there are those, who although previously successful, may have brought ego games into the session with them. They may want to provide someone else with a particular type of experience. They may be promoting some self goal. They may be nurturing negative or competitive or seductive feelings towards someone in the session. This can quickly lead to *karmic* distortions and game hallucinations. If this happens, recall the instructions. Remember the unity of all beings. One to me is shame and fame. One to me is loss or gain. Jettison your ego program and float back to the radiant bliss of at-one-ness.

If you reach the Clear Light immediately and maintain it, that is best. But if not, if you have slipped down to reality concerns, by remembering these instructions you should be able to regain what the Tibetans call the Secondary Clear Light.

While on this secondary level, an interesting dialogue occurs between pure transcendence and the awareness that this ecstatic vision is happening *to oneself*. The first radiance knows no self, no concepts. The secondary experience involves a certain state of conceptual lucidity. The knowing self hovers within that transcendent terrain from which it is usually barred. If the instructions are remembered, external reality will not intrude. But the flashing in and out between pure egoless unity, and lucid, non-game selfhood, produces an intellectual ecstasy and understanding that defies description. Previous philosophic reading will suddenly take on living meaning.

Thus in this secondary stage of the First Bardo, there is possible both the mystic non-self and the mystic self experience.

After you have experienced these two states, you may wish to pursue this distinction intellectually. We are confronted here with one of the oldest debates in Eastern philosophy. Is it better to be part of the sugar or to taste the sugar? Theological controversies and their dualities are far removed from experience. Thanks to the experimental mysticism made possible by consciousness-expanding drugs, you may have been lucky enough to have experienced the flashing back and forth between the two states. You may be lucky enough to *know* what the academic monks could only think about.

Here ends the First Bardo,
the Period of Ego-loss or Non-Game Ecstasy

Second Bardo:
The Period of Hallucinations
(Chönyid Bardo)

Introduction

If the Primary Clear Light is not recognized, there remains the possibility of maintaining the Secondary Clear Light. If that is lost, then comes the *Chönyid Bardo*, the period of *karmic* illusions or intense hallucinatory mixtures of game reality. It is very important that the instructions be remembered—they can have great influence and effect.

During this period, the flow of consciousness, microscopically clear and intense, is interrupted by fleeting attempts to rationalize and interpret. But the normal game-playing ego is not functioning effectively. There exist, therefore, unlimited possibilities for, on the one hand, delightful sensuous, intellectual and emotional novelties if one floats with the current; and, on the other hand, fearful ambuscades of confusion and terror if one tries to impose his will on the experience.

The purpose of this part of the manual is to prepare the person for the choice points which arise during this stage. Strange sounds, weird sights and disturbed visions may occur. These can awe, frighten and terrify unless one is prepared.

The experienced person will be able to maintain the recognition that all perceptions come from within and will be able to sit quietly, controlling his expanded awareness like a phantasmagoric multidimensional television set: the most acute and sensitive hallucinations—visual, auditory, touch, smell, physical and bodily; the most exquisite reactions, compassionate insight into the self, the world. The key is *inaction:* passive integration with all that occurs around you. If you try to impose your will, use your mind, rationalize, seek explanations, you will get caught in hallucinatory whirlpools.

The motto: peace, acceptance. It is all an ever-changing panorama. You are temporarily removed from the world of game. Enjoy it.

The inexperienced and those to whom ego control is important may find this passivity impossible. If you cannot remain inactive and subdue your will, then the one certain activity which can reduce panic and pull you out of hallucinatory mind-games is physical contact with another person. Go to the guide or to another participant and put your head on his lap or chest; put your face next to his and concentrate on the movement and sound of his inspiration. Breathe deeply and feel the air rush in and the sighing release. This is the oldest form of living communication; the brotherhood of breath. The guide's hand on your forehead may add to the relaxation.

Contact with another participant may be misunderstood and provoke sexual hallucinations. For this reason, helping contact should be made explicit by prearrangement. Unprepared participants may impose sexual fears or fantasies on the contact. Turn them off; they are *karmic* illusory productions.

The tender, gentle, supportive huddling together of participants is a natural development during the second phase. Do not try to rationalize this contact. Human beings and, for that matter, most all mobile terrestrial creatures have been huddling together during long, dark confused nights for several hundred thousand years.

Breathe in and breathe out with your companions. We are all one! That's what your breath is telling you.

Explanation of the Second Bardo

The underlying problem of the Second Bardo is that any and every shape—human, divine, diabolical, heroic, evil, animal, thing—which the human brain conjures up or the past life recalls, can present itself to consciousness: shapes and forms and sounds whirling by endlessly.

The underlying solution—repeated again and again—is to recognize that your brain is producing the visions. They do not exist. Nothing exists except as your consciousness gives it life.

You are standing on the threshold of recognizing the truth: there is no reality behind any of the phenomena of the ego-loss state, save the illusions stored up in your own mind either as accretions from game *(Sangsāric)* experience or as gifts from organic physical nature and its billion-year-old past history. Recognition of this truth gives liberation.

There is, of course, no way of classifying the infinite permutations and combinations of visionary elements. The cortex contains file-cards for billions of images from the history of the person, of the race, and of living forms. Any of these, at the rate of a hundred million per second (according to neurophysiologists), can flood into awareness. Bobbing around in this brilliant, symphonic sea of imagery is the remnant of the conceptual mind. On the endless watery turbulence of the Pacific Ocean bobs a tiny open mouth shouting (between saline mouthfuls), "Order! System! Explain all this!"

One cannot predict what visions will occur, nor their sequence. One can only urge the participants to shut the mouth, breathe through the nose, and turn off the fidgety, rationalizing mind. But only the experienced person of mystical bent can do this (and thus remain in serene enlightenment). The unprepared person will be confused or, worse, panicky: the intellectual struggle to control the ocean.

In order to guide the person, to help him organize his visions into explicable units, the *Chönyid Bardo* was written. There are two sections: (1) Seven Peaceful Deities with their symmetrically opposed ego traps. (2) Eight Wrathful Deities who can be joyfully accepted as visionary productions, or fled from in terror.

Each of the Seven Peaceful Deities (bisexual Father-Mother figures) are accompanied by consorts, attendants, lesser deities, saints, angels, heroes. Each of the Wrathful Deities is similarly accompanied. Lights, symbolic objects, beautiful, horrid, threatening, seething, are likewise seen.

If read literally, the *Tibetan Book of the Dead* would have you expect the "Master of All Visible Shapes" (or his opposite, the fondness for stupidity) on the first day; the "Immovable Deity of Happiness" and his consort, attendants and opposite on the second, etc. The manual should, of course, not be used rigidly, exoterically, but should be taken in its esoteric, allegorical form.

Read from this perspective, we see that the *lamas* have listed or named a thousand images which can boil up in the ever-changing jeweled mosaic of the retina (that multi-layered swamp of billions of rods and cones, infiltrated, like a Persian rug or a Mayan carving, with countless multi-colored capillaries). By preparatory reading of the manual and by its repetition during the experience, the novice is led via suggestion to recognize this fantastic retinal kaleidoscope.

Most important, he is told that they come from within. All deities and demons, all heavens and hells are internal.

The student with a particular interest in Tibetan or Tantric Buddhism should steep himself in the text of the *Chönyid Bardo*. He should obtain colored plates of the fourteen dramas of the Bardo, and he should arrange to have the guide lead him through the prescribed sequence during the drug session. This will provide an unforgettable series of liberations and will permit the devotee to emerge from the experience "reincarnated" in the *lamaist* tradition.

The aim of this manual is to make available the general outline of the Tibetan Book and to translate it into psychedelic English. For this reason we shall not present the detailed sequence of *lamaist* hallucinations but, rather, list some apparitions commonly reported by Westerners.

Following the Tibetan *Thodöl*, we have classified Second Bardo visions into seven types:

1. The Source or Creator Vision
2. The Internal Flow of Archetypal Processes
3. The Fire-Flow of Internal Unity
4. The Wave-Vibration Structure of External Forms
5. The Vibratory Waves of External Unity
6. "The Retinal Circus"
7. "The Magic Theatre"*

Visions 2 and 3 involve closed eyes and no contact with external stimuli. In Vision 2 the internal imagery is primarily conceptual. The experience can range from revelation and insight to confusion and chaos, but the cognitive, intellectual meaning is paramount. In Vision

---

*We owe the phrase "retinal circus" to Henri Michaux *(Miserable Miracle)*, and the term "magic theatre" to Hermann Hesse *(Steppenwolf)*.

3 the internal imagery is primarily emotional. The experience can range from love and ecstatic unity to fear, distrust and isolation.

Visions 4 and 5 involve open eyes and rapt attention to external stimuli, such as sounds, lights, touch, etc. In Vision 4 the external imagery is primarily conceptual and in Vision 5 emotional factors predominate.

The sevenfold table just defined bears some similarity to the *mandālic* schema of the Peaceful Deities listed for the Second Bardo in the *Tibetan Book of the Dead*.

The Peaceful Visions

Vision 1: The Source*
(Eyes closed, external stimuli ignored)

The White Light, or First Bardo energy, may be interpreted as God the Creator. The Spreader of the Seed. The Power which makes all shapes visible. Seed of all that is. Sovereign Power. The All-Powerful. The Central Sun. The One Truth. The Source of all Organic Life. The Divine Mother. The Female Creative Principle. Mother of the Space of Heaven. Radiant Father-Mother. Magnificent revelations, both spiritual and philosophic, can occur at this point marking the highest union of experience and intellect. But, because of bad *karma* (usually religious beliefs of a monotheistic or punitive nature), the glorious light of the seed wisdom can produce awe and terror. The person will wish to flee and will beget a fondness for the dull white light symbolizing stupidity.

Persons from a Judaeo-Christian background conceive of an enormous gulf between divinity (which is "up there") and the self ("down here"). Christian mystics' claims to unity with divine radiance has always posed problems for theologians who are committeed to the cosmological subject-object distinction. Most Westerners, therefore, find it difficult to attain unity with the source-light.

If the guide ascertains that the voyager is struggling with thoughts or feelings about the creative source energy, he can read the appropriate instructions (page 102).

Vision 2: The Internal Flow of Archetypal Processes
(Eyes closed, external stimuli ignored; intellectual aspects)

If the undifferentiated light of the First Bardo or of the Source Energy is lost, luminous waves of differentiated forms can flood through the consciousness. The person's mind begins to identify

---

*The first Peaceful Deity listed by the *Bardo Thödol* is the *Bhagavan Vairochana* who occupies the center of the *mandala* of the five *Dhyānī-Buddhas*. His attributes of source-power have been translated into those of the monotheistic creator of Western religions.

these figures, that is, to label them and experience revelations about the life process.*

Specifically, the subject is caught up in an endless flow of colored forms, microbiological shapes, cellular acrobatics, capillary whirling. The cortex is tuned in on molecular processes which are completely new and strange: a Niagara of abstract designs; the life-stream flowing, flowing.

These visions might perhaps be described as pure sensations of cellular and sub-cellular processes. It is uncertain whether they involve the retina and/or the visual cortex, or whether they are flashes of direct, molecular sensation in other areas of the central nervous system. They are subjectively described as internal visions.

Another class of internal process images involves sound. Again we do not know whether these sensations originate in the auditory apparatus and/or in the auditory cortex, or whether they are flashes of direct molecular sensations in other areas. They are subjectively described as internal sounds: clicking, thudding, clashing, soughing, ringing, tapping, moaning, shrill whistles.† These noises, like the vi-

---

*Lama Govinda tells us that *Amoghasiddhi* represents ". . . the mysterious activity of spiritual forces, which work removed from the senses, invisible and imperceptible, with the aim of guiding the individual (or, more properly: all living beings) towards the maturity of knowledge and liberation. The yellow light of an (inner) sun invisible to human eyes . . . (in which the unfathomable space of the universe seems to open itself) for the serene mystic green of *Amoghasiddhi*. . . . On the elementary plane this all-pervading power corresponds to the element air—the principle of movement and extension, of life and breath *(prāna)*." Lama Govinda: *Foundations of Tibetan Mysticism*. London: E. P. Dutton & Co., Inc., 1959, p. 120.

The fifth day of the *Bardo Thödol* confronts the deceased with the *Bhagavān Buddha Amoghasiddhi*, Almighty Conqueror, from the green Northern realm of Successful Performance of Best Actions, attended by a Divine Mother, and two *Bodhisattvas* representing the mental functions of "equilibrium, immutability, and almighty power" and "clearer of obscurations."

†The Tibetan Book includes a brilliant discussion of internal process noises. ". . . innumerable (other) kinds of musical instruments, filling (with music) the whole world-systems and causing them to vibrate, to quake and tremble with sounds so mighty as to daze one's brain. . . ."

"Tibetan *lamas*, in chanting their rituals, employ seven (or eight) sorts of musical instruments: big drums, cymbals (commonly of brass), conch shells, bells (like the handbells used in the Christian Mass Service), timbrels, small clarionets (sounding like Highland bagpipes), big trumpets, and human thighbone trumpets. Although the com-

sions, are direct sensations unencumbered by mental concepts. Raw, molecular, dancing units of energy.

The mind sweeps in and out of this evolutionary stream, creating cosmological revelations. Dozens of mythical and Darwinian insights flash into awareness. The person is allowed to glance back down the flow of time and to perceive how the life energy continually manifests itself in forms, transient, always changing, reforming. Microscopic forms merge with primal creative myths. The mirror of consciousness is held up to the life stream.

As long as the person floats with the current, he is exposed to a billion-year lesson in cosmology. But the drag of the mind is always present. The tendency to impose arbitrary, isolating order on the organic process.

Sometimes the voyager feels he should report back his visions. He converts the life flow into a cosmic ink-blot test—attempts to label each form. "Now I see a peacock's tail. Now Muslim knights in colored armor. Oh, now a waterfall of jewels. Now, Chinese music. Now, gem-like serpents, etc." Verbalizations of this sort dull the light, stop the flow and should not be encouraged.

Another trap is that of imposing a sexual interpretation. The dancing, playful flow of life is, in the most reverent sense, sexual. Forms merging, spinning together, reproducing. Eros in its countless manifestations. The Tibetans refer to the female Bodhisattvas Pushpema, personification of blossoms, and Lasema, the "Belle", depicted holding a mirror in a coquettish attitude. Keep the pure, spontaneous awareness

---

bined sounds of these instruments are far from being melodious, the *lamas* maintain that they psychically produce in the devotee an attitude of deep veneration and faith, because they are the counterparts of the natural sounds which one's own body is heard producing when the fingers are put in the ears to shut out external sounds. Stopping the ears thus, there are heard a thudding sound, like that of a big drum being beaten: a clashing sound, as of cymbals; a soughing sound, as of a wind moving through a forest—as when a conch-shell is blown; a ringing as of bells; a sharp tapping sound, as when a timbrel is used; a moaning sound, like that of a clarionet; a bass moaning sound, as if made with a big trumpet; and a shriller sound, as of a thigh-bone trumpet.

"Not only is this interesting as a theory of Tibetan sacred music, but it gives the clue to the esoteric interpretation of the symbolical natural sounds of Truth (referred to in the second paragraph following, and elsewhere in our text), which are said to be, or to proceed from, the intellectual faculties within the human mentality."—(Evans-Wentz, p. 128)

of the Mirror-like Wisdom. Laugh joyously at the tricks of the life process, forever decking out forms in seductive, enticing patterns to keep the dance going. If the voyager interprets the visions of Eros in terms of his personal sexual game model, and attempts to think or plan—"what should I do? what role should I play?"—he is likely to slip down into the Third Bardo. Sexual plots dominate his awareness, the flow fades, the mirror tarnishes, and he is rudely reborn as a confused, thinking being.

Still another impasse is the imposition of physical symptom games upon the biological flow. The new somatic sensations may be interpreted as symptoms. If it is new, it must be bad. Any organ of the body may be selected as the focus of the "illness." People whose primary expectation when taking a psychedelic substance is medical, are particularly likely to fall into this trap. Medical doctors are, in fact, extremely prone and can imagine colorful diseases and fatal attacks.

In the case of the most widely-used psychedelics (LSD, psilocybin, etc.), it is safe to say that such bodily effects are virtually never the direct effect of the drug. The drug acts only on the brain and activates *central* neural patterns. All physical symptoms are created by the mind. Bodily sickness is a sign that the ego is fighting to maintain or regain its hold over an outpouring of feeling, over a dissolution of emotional boundaries.

If the person complains of *physical symptoms* such as nausea or pain, the guide should read him the instructions for physical symptoms (page 103).

The negative, wrathful counterpart to this vision occurs if the voyager reacts with fear to the powerful flow of life forms. Such a reaction is attributable to the cumulated result of game playing *(karma)* dominated by anger or stupidity. A nightmarish hell-world may ensue. The visual forms appear like a confusing chaos of cheap, ugly dimestore objects, brassy, vulgar and useless. The person may become terrified at the prospect of being engulfed by them. The awesome sounds may be heard as hideous, clashing, oppressive, grating noises. The person will attempt to escape from these perceptions into restless external activity (talking, moving around, etc.) or into conceptual, analytic, mental activity.

The experience is the same, the intellectual interpretation is different. Instead of revelation, there is confusion; instead of calm joy, there is fear. The guide, recognizing the voyager to be in such a state, can help him get free, by reading the instructions for Vision 2 (page 104).

Vision 3: The Fire-Flow of Internal Unity
(Eyes closed, external stimuli ignored, emotional aspects)

The First Bardo instructions should keep you face-to-face with the void-ecstasy. Yet there are classes of men who, having carried over *karmic* conflict about feeling-inhibition, prove unable to hold the pure experience beyond all feelings, and slip into emotionally toned visions. The undifferentiated energy of the First Bardo is woven into visionary games in the form of intense feelings. Exquisite, intense, pulsating sensations of unity and love will be felt; the negative counterpart is feelings of attachment, greed, isolation and bodily concerns.

It comes about this way: the pure flow of energy loses its white void quality and becomes sensed as intense feelings. An emotional game is imposed. Incredible new physical sensations pulse through the body. The glow of life is felt flooding along veins. One merges into a unitive ocean of orgastic, fluid electricity,* the endless flow of shared-life, of love.

Visions related to the circulatory system are common. The subject tumbles down through his own arterial network. The motor of the heart reverberates as one with the pulsing of all life. The heart then breaks, and red fire bleeds out to merge with all living beings. All living organisms are throbbing together. One is joyfully aware of the

---

*The Peaceful Deity of the *Bardo Thödol* personifying this vision is the *Buddha Amitabbha*, the all-discriminating wisdom of feeling, boundless light, representing life eternal. Lama Govinda writes that "The deep red light of discriminating inner vision shines forth from his heart . . . fire corresponds to him and thus, according to the ancient traditional symbolism, the eye and the function of seeing." (Govinda, *op. cit.*, p. 120.) With the *Bhagavān Amitabbha* comes the Bodhisattva *Chenrazee*, embodiment of mercy or compassion, the great pitier ever on the lookout to discover distress and to succour the troubled. He is joined by the *Bodhisattva* "Glorious Gentle-voiced One," and the female incarnates "song" and "light."

two-billion-year-old electric sexual dance; one is at last divested of robot clothes and limbs and undulates in the endless chain of living forms.

Dominating this ecstatic state is the feeling of intense love. You are a joyful part of all life. The memory of former delusions of self-hood and differentiation invokes exultant laughter.

All the harsh, dry, brittle angularity of game life is melted. You drift off — soft, rounded, moist, warm. Merged with all life. You may feel yourself floating out and down into a warm sea. Your individuality and autonomy of movement are moistly disappearing. Your control is surrendered to the total organism. Blissful passivity. Ecstatic, orgiastic, undulating unity. All worries and concerns wash away. All is gained as everything is given up. There is organic revelation. Every cell in your body is singing its song of freedom — the entire biological universe is in harmony, liberated from the censorship and control of you and your restricted ambitions.

But wait! You, YOU, are disappearing into the unity. You are being swallowed up by the ecstatic undulation. Your ego, that one tiny remaining strand of self, screams STOP! You are terrified by the pull of the glorious, dazzling, transparent, radiant red light. You wrench yourself out of the life-flow, drawn by your intense attachment to your old desires. There is a terrible rending as your roots tear out of the life matrix — a ripping of your fibres and veins away from the greater body to which you were attached. And when you have cut yourself off from the fire-flow of life the throbbing stops, the ecstasy ceases, your limbs harden and stiffen into angular forms, your plastic doll body has regained its orientation. There you sit, isolated from the stream of life, impotent master of your desires and appetites, miserable.

While you are floating down the evolutionary river, there comes a sense of limitless self-less power. The delight of flowing cosmic belongingness. The astounding discovery that consciousness can tune in to an infinite number of organic levels. There are billions of cellular processes in your body, each with its universe of experience — an endless variety of ecstasies. The simple joys and pains and burdens of your ego represent one set of experiences — a repetitious, dusty set. As you slip into the fire-flow of biological energy, series after series of experiential sets flash by. You are no longer encapsulated in the structure of ego and tribe.

But through panic and a desire to latch on to the familiar, you shut off the flow, open your eyes; then the flowingness is lost. The potentiality to move from one level of consciousness to another is gone. Your fear and desire to control have driven you to settle for one static site of consciousness. To use the Eastern or genetic metaphor, you have frozen the dance of energy and committed yourself to one incarnation, and you have done it out of fear.

When this happens, there are several steps which can take you back to the biological flow (and from there to the First Bardo). First, close your eyes. Lie on your stomach and let your body sink through the floor, merge with the surroundings. Feel the hard, square edges of your body soften and start to move in the bloodstream. Let the rhythm of breathing become tide flow. Bodily contact is probably the most effective method of softening hardened surfaces. No movement. No body games. Close physical contact with another invariably brings about the unity of fire-flow. Your blood begins to flow into the other's body. His breathing pours into your lungs. You both drift down the capillary river.

Another form of life process images is the flow of auditory sensations. The endless series of abstract sounds (described in the preceding vision) bounce through awareness. The emotional reaction to these can be neutral or can involve intense feelings of unity, or of annoyed fear.

The positive reaction occurs when the subject merges with the sound flow. The thudding drum of the heart is sensed as the basic anthem of humanity. The whooshing sough of the breath as the rushing river of all life. Overwhelming feelings of love, gratitude and oneness funnel into the moment of sound, into each note of the biological concerto.

But, as always, the voyager may intrude his personality with its wants and opinions. He may not "like" the noise. His judgmental ego may be aesthetically offended by the sounds of life. The heart thud is, after all, monotonous; the natural music of the inner ear, with its clicks and hums and whistles, lacks the romantic symmetries of Beethoven. The terrible separation of "me" from my body occurs. Horrible. Out of my control. Turn it off.

The trained guide can usually sense when ego-attachment threatens to pull the person out of the unitive flow. At this time he can guide the voyager by reading the instructions for Vision 3 (page 105).

Vision 4: The Wave-Vibration Structure of External Forms
(Eyes open or rapt involvement with external stimuli; intellectual aspects)

The pure, content-free light of the First Bardo probably involves basic electrical wave energy. This is nameless, indescribable, because it is far beyond any concepts which we now possess. Some future atomic physicist may be able to classify this energy. Perhaps it will always be ineffable for a nervous system such as that of *homo sapiens*. Can an organic system "comprehend" the vastly more efficient inorganic? At any event, most persons, even the most illuminated, find it impossible to maintain experiential contact with this void-light and slip back to imposing mental structures, hallucinatory and revelatory, upon the flow.

Thus we are brought to another frequent vision which involves intense, rapt, unitive awareness of external stimuli. If the eyes are open, this super-reality effect can be visual. The penetrating impact of other stimuli can also set off revelatory imagery.

It comes about this way. The subject's awareness is suddenly invaded by an outside stimulus. His attention is captured, but his old conceptual mind is not functioning. But other sensitivities are engaged. He experiences direct sensation. The raw "is-ness." He sees, not objects, but patterns of light waves. He hears, not "music" or "meaningful" sound, but acoustic waves. He is struck with the sudden revelation that all sensation and perception are based on wave vibrations. That the world around him which heretofore had an illusory solidity, is nothing more than a play of physical waves. That he is involved in a cosmic television show which has no more substantiality that the images on his TV picture tube.*

---

*The Peaceful Diety of the *Thödol* personifying this vision is *Akshobhya*. According to Lama Govinda, "In the light of the Mirror-like Wisdom . . . things are freed from their "thingness," their isolation, without being deprived of their form; they are divested of their materiality, without being dissolved, because the creative principle of the mind, which is at the bottom of all form and materiality, is recognized as the active side of the universal Store Consciousness *(alaya-vijnana)*, on the surface of which forms arise and pass away, like the waves on the surface of the ocean. . . ." (Govinda, *op. cit.,* p. 119.)

The atomic structure of matter is, of course, known to us intellectually, but never experienced by the adult except in states of intense altered consciousness. Learning from a physics textbook about the wave structure of matter is one thing. Experiencing it—being in it—with the old, familiar, gross, hallucinatory comfort of "solid" things gone and unavailable, is quite another matter.

If these super-real visions involve wave phenomena, then the external world takes on a radiance and a revelation that is staggeringly clear. The experienced insight that the world of phenomena exists in the form of waves, electronic images, can produce a sense of illuminated power. Everything is experienced as consciousness.

These exultant radiations should be recognized as productions of your own internal processes. You should not attempt to control or conceptualize. This can come later. There is the danger of hallucinatory freezing. The subject rushes back (sometimes literally) to the three-dimensional reality, convinced of the fixed "truth" of one experienced revelation. Many misguided mystics and many persons called insane have fallen into this ambuscade. This is like making a still photograph of a television pattern and shouting that one has finally seized the truth. All is ecstatic electric *Māyā*, the two-billion-year dance of waves. No one part of it is more real than another. Everything at all moments is shimmering with all the meaning.

So far we have considered the positive radiance of clarity; but there are fearful negative aspects of the fourth vision. When the subject senses that his "world" is fragmenting into waves, he may become terrified. "He," "me," "I" are dissolving! The world around me is supposed to sit, static and dead, quietly awaiting my manipulation. But these passive things have changed into a shimmering dance of living energy! The *Māyā* nature of phenomena creates panic. Where is the solid base? Every thing, every concept, every form upon which one rests one's mind collapses into electrical vibrations lacking solidity.

The face of the guide or of one's beloved friend becomes a dancing mosaic of impulses on one's cortex. "My consciousness" has created everything of which I am conscious. I have kinescoped my world, my loved ones, myself. All are just shimmering energy patterns. Instead of clarity and exultant power, there is confusion. The subject staggers around, grasping at electron-patterns, striving to freeze them back into the familiar robot forms.

All solidity is gone. All phenomena are paper images pasted on the glass screen of consciousness. For the unprepared, or for the person whose *karmic* residue stresses control, the discovery of the wave-nature of all structure, the *Māyā* revelation, is a disastrous web of uncertainty.

We have discussed only the visual aspects of the fourth vision. Auditory phenomena are of equal importance. Here the solid, labelled nature of auditory patterns is lost, and the mechanical impact of sound hitting the eardrum is registered. In some cases, sound becomes converted into pure sensation, and synesthesia (mixture of sense modalities) occurs. Sounds are experienced as colors. External sensations hitting the cortex are recorded as molecular events, ineffable.

The most dramatic auditory visions occur with music. Just as any object radiates a pattern of electrons and can become the essence of all energy, so can any note of music be sensed as naked energy trembling in space, timeless. The movement of notes, like the shuttling of oscillograph beams. Each capturing all energy, the electric core of the universe. Nothing existing except the needle-clear resonance on the tympanic membrane. Unforgettable revelations about the nature of reality occur at these moments.

But the hellish interpretation is also possible. As the learned structure of sound collapses, the direct impact of waves can be sensed as noise. For one who is compelled to institute order, his order, on the world around him, it is at least annoying and often disturbing to have the raw tattoo of sound resonating in consciousness.

Noise! What an irreverent concept. Is not everything noise; all sensation the divine pattern of wave energy, meaningless only to those who insist on imposing their own meaning?

Preparation is the key to a serene passage through this visionary territory. The subject who has studied this manual will be able, when face to face with the phenomenon, to recognize and flow with it.

The sensitive guide will be ready to pick up on any cue that the subject is wandering in the fourth vision. If the voyager's eyes are open (indicating visual reactions), he can read the instructions for Vision 4 (page 106).

If the guide senses that the voyager is experiencing the fragmentation of external sound into wave vibrations, he can amend the instructions appropriately (changing the visual references to auditory).

Vision 5: The Vibratory Waves of External Unity
(Eyes open, or rapt involvement with external stimuli; emotional aspects)

As the learned perceptions disappear and the structure of the external world disintegrates into direct wave phenomena, the aim is to maintain a pure, content-free awareness (First Bardo). Despite the preparations, one is likely to be led backwards by one's own mental inclinations into two hallucinatory or revelatory interpretations of reality. One reaction leads to the intellectual clarity or frightened confusion of the fourth vision (just described). Another interpretation is the emotional reaction to the fragmentation of differentiated forms. One can be engulfed in ecstatic unity, or one can slip into isolated egotism. The *Bardol Thödol* calls the former the "Wisdom of Equality" and the latter the "quagmire of worldly existence accruing from violent egotism."* In the state of radiant unity, one senses that there is only one network of energy in the universe and that all things and all sentient beings are momentary manifestations of the single pattern. When egotistic interpretations are imposed on the fifth vision, the "plastic doll" phenomena are experienced. Differentiated forms are seen as inorganic, dull, mass-produced, shabby, plastic, and all persons (including self) are seen as lifeless mannequins isolated from the vibrant dance of energy, which has been lost.

The experiential data of this vision are similar to that of the fourth vision. All artifactual learned structure collapses back to energy vibrations. The awareness is dominated not by revelatory clarity but by

---

*The Peaceful Deity of the fifth vision comes in the form of the *Bhagavān Ratnasambhava*, born of a jewel. He is embraced by the Divine Mother. She of the Buddha Eyes, and accompanied by the *Bodhisattvas*, womb of the sky. All-good, and those holding incense and rosary. "On the elementary plane *Ratnasambhava* corresponds to the earth, which carries and nourishes all beings with the equanimity and patience of a mother, in whose eyes all beings, borne by her, are equal." (Govinda, *op. cit.*, p. 119.)

shimmering unity. The subject is entranced by the silent, whirling play of forces. Exquisite forms dance by him, all surrounding objects radiate energy, brilliant emanations. His own body is seen as a play of forces. If he looks in a mirror, he sees a shining mosaic of particles. The sense of his own wave structure becomes stronger. A feeling of melting, floating off. The body is no longer a separate unit but a cluster of vibrations sending and receiving energy—a phase of the dance of energy which has been going on for millennia.

A sense of profound one-ness, a feeling of the unity of all energy. Superficial differences of role, cast, status, sex, species, form, power, size, beauty, even the distinctions between inorganic and living energy, disappear before the ecstatic union of all in one. All gestures, words, acts and events are equivalent in value—all are manifestations of the one consciousness which pervades everything. "You," "I" and "he" are gone, "my" thoughts are "ours," "your" feelings are "mine." Communication is unnecessary, since complete communion exists. A person can sense another's feeling and mood directly, as if they were his own. By a glance, whole lifetimes and words can be transmitted. If all are at peace, the vibrations are "in phase." If there is discord, "out of phase" vibrations will be set up which will be felt like discordant music. Bodies melt into waves. Objects in the environment—lights, trees, plants, flowers—seem to open and welcome you: they are part of you. You are both simply different pulses of the same vibrations. A pure feeling of ecstatic harmony with all beings is the keynote of this vision.

But as before, terrors can occur. Unity requires ecstatic self-sacrifice. Loss of ego brings fright to the unprepared. The fragmentation of form into waves can bring the most terrible fear known to man: the ultimate epistemological revelation.

The fact of the matter is that all apparent forms of matter and body are momentary clusters of energy. We are little more than flickers on a multidimensional television screen. This realization directly experienced can be delightful. You suddenly wake up from the delusion of separate form and hook up to the cosmic dance. Consciousness slides along the wave matrices, silently at the speed of light.

The terror comes with the discovery of transience. Nothing is fixed, no form solid. Everything you can experience is "nothing but" electrical waves. You feel ultimately tricked. A victim of the great television producer. Distrust. The people around you are lifeless television robots. The world around you is a facade, a stage set. You are a helpless marionette, a plastic doll in a plastic world.

If others attempt to help, they are seen as wooden, waxen, feelingless, cold, grotesque, maniacal, space-fiction monsters. You are unable to feel. "I am dead. I will never live and feel again." In wild panic you may attempt to force feeling back—by action, by shouting. You will then enter the Third Bardo stage and be reborn in an unpleasant way.

The best method to escape from fifth vision terrors is to remember this manual, relax, and swing with the wave dance. Or to communicate to the guide that you are in a plastic doll phase, and he will guide you back.

Another solution is to move to the internal biological flow. Follow the instructions given in the third vision: close your eyes, lie prone, seek bodily contact, float down into your bodily stream. In so doing, you are recapitulating the evolutionary sequence. For billions of years, inorganic energy danced the cosmic round before the biological rhythm began. Don't rush it.

If the guide senses that the person is experiencing plastic doll visions or is afraid of the uncontrollability of his own feelings, he should read to him the instructions for Vision 5 (page 107).

Vision 6: "The Retinal Circus"

Each of the Second Bardo visions thus far described was one aspect of the "experiencing of reality." The inner fire or outer waves, apprehended intellectually or emotionally—each vision with its correspondent traps. Each of the "Peaceful Deities" appears with its attendant "Wrathful Deities." To maintain any of these visions for any length of time requires a certain degree of concentration or "one-pointedness" of mind, as well as the ability to recognize them and not to be afraid. Thus, for most persons, the experience may pass through one or more of these phases without the voyager being able to hold them or stay with them. He may open and close his eyes, he may become alternately absorbed in internal sensations and external forms. The experience may be chaotic, beautiful, thrilling, incomprehensible, magical, ever-changing.*

He will travel freely through many worlds of experience—from direct contact with life-process forms and images, he may pass to visions of human game-forms. He may see and understand with unimagined clarity and brilliance various social and self-games that he and others play. His own struggles in *karmic* (game) existence will appear pitiful and laughable. Ecstatic freedom of consciousness is the keynote of this vision. Exploration of unimagined realms. Theatrical adventures. Plays within plays within plays. Symbols change into things symbolized and vice versa. Words become things, thoughts are music, music is smelled, sounds are touched, complete interchangeability of the senses.

All things are possible. All feelings are possible. A person may "try on" various moods like so many pieces of clothing. Subjects and objects whirl, transform, change into each other, merge, fuse, disperse again. External objects dance and sing. The mind plays upon them as upon a musical instrument. They assume any form, significance or quality upon command. They are admired, adored, analyzed, examined, changed, made beautiful or ugly, large or small, important or trivial, useful, dangerous, magical or incomprehensible. They may be reacted to with wonder, amazement, humor, veneration, love, disgust, fascination, horror, delight, fear, ecstasy.

Like a computer with unlimited access to any programs, the mind roams freely. Personal and racial memories bubble up to the surface of consciousness, inter-play with fantasies, wishes, dreams and external objects. A present event becomes charged with profound emotional significance, a cosmic phenomenon becomes identical with some personal quirk. Metaphysical problems are juggled and bounced around. Pure "primary process," spontaneous outpouring of association, oppo-

*In the *Bardo Thödol*, on the sixth day appear the radiant lights of the combined Five Wisdoms of the *Dhyānī-Buddhas*, the protective deities (gatekeepers of the *mandala*) and the Buddhas of the Six Realms of game-existence. According to Lama Govinda: "The Inner Way of *Vajra-Sattva*, consists in the combination of the rays of the Wisdoms of the four *Dhyānī-Buddhas* and their absorption within one's own heart—in other words, in the recognition that all these radiances are the emanations of one's own mind in a state of perfect tranquillity and serenity, a state in which the mind reveals its true universal nature." (Govinda, *op., cit.*, p. 262.)

sites merging, images fusing, condensing, shifting, collapsing, expanding, merging, connecting.

This kaleidoscopic vision of game-reality may be frightening and confusing to an ill-prepared subject. Instead of exquisite clarity of many-levelled perception, he will experience a confused chaos of uncontrollable, meaningless forms. Instead of delight at the playful acrobatics of the free intellect, there will be anxious clinging to an elusive order. Morbid and scatological hallucinations may occur, evoking disgust and shame.

As before, this negative vision occurs only if the person attempts to control or rationalize the magic panorama. Relax and accept whatever comes. Remember that all visions are created by your mind, the happy and the unhappy, the beautiful and the ugly, the delightful and the horrifying. Your consciousness is creator, performer and spectator of the "retinal circus."

If the guide senses that the voyager is in or seems to be in the "retinal circus" vision, he may read to him the appropriate instructions (page 108).

Vision 7: "The Magic Theatre"

If the voyager was unable to maintain the passive serenity necessary for the contemplation of the previous visions (the peaceful deities), he moves now into a more dramatic and active phase. The play of forms and things becomes the play of heroic figures, superhuman spirits and demigods.* You may see radiating figures in human forms. The "Lo-

---

*In the Tibetan Handbook, this is described as the vision of the five "Knowledge-Holding Deities," arranged in the form of a *mandala*, each embraced by *Dākinīs*. in an ecstatic dance. The Knowledge-holding Deities symbolize "the highest level of individual or humanly conceivable knowledge, as attained in the consciousness of great Yogis. inspired thinkers or similar heroes of the spirit. They represent the last step before the "breaking-through" towards the universal consciousness—or the first on the return from there to the plane of human knowledge." (Govinda, *op. cit.,* p. 202.) The *Dākinīs* are female embodiments of knowledge, representing the inspirational impulses of consciousness leading to break-through. The other four Knowledge-Holders, besides the central Lord of Dance, are: the Knowledge-holder abiding in the earth, the Knowledge-holder who has power over the duration of life, the Knowledge-holder of the Great Symbol, and the Knowledge-holder of Spontaneous Realization.

tus Lord of Dance": the supreme image of a demi-god who perceives the effects of all actions. The prince of movement, dancing in an ecstatic embrace with his female counterpart. Heroes, heroines, celestial warriors, male and female demi-gods, angels, fairies—the exact form of these figures will depend on the person's background and tradition. Archetypal figures in the forms of characters from Greek, Egyptian, Nordic, Celtic, Aztec, Persian, Indian, Chinese mythology. The shapes differ, the source is the same: they are the concrete embodiments of aspects of the person's own psyche. Archetypal forces below verbal awareness and expressible only in symbolic form. The figures are often extremely colorful and accompanied by a variety of awe-inspiring sounds. If the voyager is prepared and in a relaxed, detached frame of mind, he is exposed to a fascinating and dazzling display of dramatic creativity. The Cosmic Theatre. The Divine Comedy. If his eyes are open, he may visualize the other voyagers as representing these figures. The face of a friend may turn into that of a young boy, a baby, the child-god; into a heroic statue, a wise old man; a woman, animal, goddess, sea-mother, young girl, nymph, elf, goblin, leprechaun. Images of the great painters arise as the familiar representations of these spirits. The images are inexhaustible and manifold. An illuminating voyage into the areas where the personal consciousness merges with the supra-individual.

The danger is that the voyager becomes frightened by or unduly attracted to these powerful figures. The forces represented by them may be more intense than he was prepared for. Inability or unwillingness to recognize them as products of one's own mind, leads to escape into animalistic pursuits. The person may become involved in the pursuit of power, lust, wealth and descend into Third Bardo rebirth struggles.

If the guide senses that the voyager is caught in this trap, the appropriate instructions may be used (page 109).

The Wrathful Visions

(Second Bardo Nightmares)

Seven Second Bardo visions have been described. At each one of them, the voyager could recognize what he saw and be liberated. Multitudes will be liberated by that recognition; and although multitudes obtain liberation in that manner, the number of sentient beings being great, evil *karma* powerful, obscurations dense, propensities of too long standing, the Wheel of Ignorance and Illusion becomes neither exhausted nor accelerated. Despite the confrontations, there is a vast preponderance of those who wander downwards unliberated.

Thus, in the Tibetan *Thödol*, after the seven peaceful deities, there come seven visions of wrathful deities, fifty-eight in number, male and female, "flame-enhaloed, wrathful, blood-drinking." These *Herukas* as they are called, will not be described in detail, especially since Westerners are liable to experience the wrathful deities in different forms. Instead of many-headed fierce mythological demons, they are more likely to be engulfed and ground by impersonal machinery, manipulated by scientific, torturing control-devices and other space-fiction horrors.*

The Tibetans regard the nightmare visions as primarily intellectual products. They assign them to the Brain *chakra*, whereas the peaceful deities are assigned to the Heart *chakra* and the Knowledge-Holding deities to the intermediate Throat *chakra*. They are the reactions of the mind to the process of consciousness-expansion. They represent the attempts of the intellect to maintain its threatened boundaries. They sym-

---

*Some general remarks about the Tibetan interpretation of these visions. The Wrathful Deities are regarded as "only the former Peaceful Deities in changed aspect." Lama Govinda writes: "The peaceful forms of *Dhyānī-Buddhas* represent the highest ideal of Buddhahood in its completed, final, static condition of ultimate attainment or perfection, seen retrospectively as it were, as a state of complete rest and harmony. The Herukas, on the other hand, which are described as "blood-drinking," angry or "terrifying" deities— are merely the dynamic aspect of enlightenment, the process of becoming a Buddha, of attaining illumination, as symbolized by the Buddha's struggle with the Hosts of *Māra* . . . The ecstatic figures, heroic and terrifying, express the act of breaking through towards the unthinkable, the intellectually "Unattainable." They represent the leap over the chasm, which yawns between an intellectual surface consciousness and the intuitive suprapersonal depth-consciousness." (Govinda, *op. cit.*, pp. 198, 202.)

bolize the struggle of breaking through to ego-loss understanding and awareness.

Because of the terror and awe they produce, recognition is difficult. Yet in a way it is also easier in that, since these negative hallucinations command all attention, the mind is alert and therefore through trying to escape from fear and terror, people get involved in psychotic states and suffer. But with the aid of this manual and the presence of a guide, the voyager will recognize these hell visions as soon as he sees them, and welcome them like old friends.

Again, when psychologists, philosophers, and psychiatrists, who do not know these teachings, experience ego-loss—however assiduously they may have devoted themselves to academic study and however clever they may have been in expounding intellectual theories—none of the higher phenomena will appear. This is because they are unable to *recognize* the visions occurring in these psychedelic experiences. Suddenly seeing something they had never seen before and possessing no intellectual concepts, they view it as inimical; and, antagonistic feelings arising, they pass into miserable states. Thus, if one has not had practical experience with these teachings, the radiances and lights will not appear.

Those who believe in these doctrines even though they may seem to be unrefined, irregular in performance of duties, inelegant in habits, and perhaps even unable to practice the doctrine successfully—let no one doubt them or be disrespectful towards them, but pay reverence to their mystic faith. That alone will enable them to attain liberation. Elegance and efficiency of devotional practice are not necessary—just acquaintance with and trust in these teachings.

Well-prepared persons need not experience Second Bardo hell visions at all. Right from the beginning they can pass into paradisiacal states led by heroes, heroines, angels and super-spirits. "They will merge into rainbow radiance; there will be sun-showers, sweet scent of incense in the air, music in the skies, radiances."

This manual is indispensable to those students who are unprepared. Those proficient in meditation will recognize the Clear Light at the moment of ego-loss and will enter the Blissful Void (*Dharma-Kāya*). They will also recognize the positive and negative visions of the Second Bardo and obtain illumination *(Sambhogha-Kāya)*; and being re-born on a higher level will become inspired saints or teachers *(Nirmına-Kāya). The study and pursuit of enlightenment can always be taken up again at the point where it was broken by the last ego-loss, thus ensuring continuity of karma.*

By the use of this manual, enlightenment can be obtained without meditation, through hearing alone. It can liberate even very heavy ego-game players. The distinction between those who know it and those who do not becomes very clear. Enlightenment follows instantly. Those who have been reached by it cannot have prolonged negative experiences.

The teaching concerning the hell-visions is the same as before; recognize them to be your own thought-forms, relax, float downstream. The instructions on page 110 may be read. If, after this, recognition is still impossible and liberation is not obtained, then the voyager will descend into the Third Bardo, the Period of Re-Entry.

Conclusion of Second Bardo

However much experience one may have had, there is always the possibility of delusions occurring in these psychedelic states. Those with practice in meditation recognize the truth as soon as the experience begins. Reading this manual beforehand is important. Having some degree of self-knowledge is helpful at the moment of ego-death.

Meditation on the various positive and negative archetypal forms is very important for Second Bardo phases. Therefore, read this manual, keep it, remember it, bear it in mind, read it regularly; let the words and meanings be very clear; they should not be forgotten, even under extreme duress. It is called "The Great Liberation by Hearing" because even those with selfish deeds on their conscience can be liberated if they hear it. If heard only once, it can be efficacious because even though not understood, it will be remembered during the psychedelic state, since the mind is more lucid then. It should be proclaimed to all living persons; it should be read over the pillows of ill persons; it should be read to dying persons; it should be broadcast.

Those who meet this doctrine are fortunate. It is not easy to encounter. Even when read, it is difficult to comprehend. *Liberation will be won simply through not disbelieving it upon hearing it.*

Here ends the Second Bardo,
the Period of Hallucinations

Third Bardo:
The Period of Re-entry
(Sidpa Bardo)

Introduction

If, in the second Bardo, the voyager is incapable of holding on to the knowledge that the peaceful and wrathful visions were projections of his own mind, but became attracted to or frightened by one or more of them, he will enter the Third Bardo. In this period he struggles to regain routine reality and his ego; the Tibetans call it the Bardo of "seeking rebirth." It is the period in which the consciousness makes the transition from transcendent reality to the reality of ordinary waking life. The teachings of this manual are of the utmost importance if one wishes to make a peaceful and enlightened re-entry and avoid a violent or unpleasant one.

In the original *Bardo Thödol* the aim of the teachings is "liberation," i.e., release from the cycle of birth and death. Interpreted esoterically, this means that the aim is to remain at the stage of perfect illumination and not to return to social game reality.

Only persons of extremely advanced spiritual development are able to accomplish this, by exercising the Transference Principle at the moment of ego-death. For average persons who undertake a psychedelic voyage, the return to game reality is inevitable. Such persons can and should use this part of the manual for the following purposes:

1. To free themselves from Third Bardo traps
2. To prolong the session, thus assuring a maximum
   degree of illumination
3. To select a favorable re-entry, i.e., to return to a wiser
   and more peaceful post-session personality

Although no definite time estimates can be given, the Tibetans esti-mate that about 50 percent of the entire psychedelic experience is spent in the Third Bardo by most normal people. At times, as indicated in the Introduction, someone may move straight to the re-entry period if he is unprepared for or frightened by the ego-loss experiences of the first two Bardos.

The types of re-entry made can profoundly color the person's subse-quent attitudes and feelings about himself and the world, for weeks or even months afterwards. A session which has been predominantly neg-ative and fearful can still be turned to great advantage and much can be learned from it, provided the re-entry is positive and highly con-scious. Conversely, a happy and revelatory experience can be made valueless by a fearful or negative re-entry.

The key instructions of the Third Bardo are: (1) *do nothing*, stay calm, passive and relaxed, no matter what happens; and (2) *recognize* where you are. If you do not recognize you will be driven by fear to make a premature and unfavorable re-entry. Only by recognizing can you main-tain that state of calm, passive concentration necessary for a favorable re-entry. That is why so many recognition-points are given. If you fail on one, it is always possible, up to the very end, to succeed on another. Hence these teachings should be read carefully and remembered well.

In the following sections some of the characteristic Third Bardo ex-periences are described. In Part IV instructions are given appropriate to each section. At this stage in a psychedelic session the voyager is usually capable of telling the guide verbally what he is experiencing, so that the appropriate sections can be read. A wise guide can often sense the precise nature of the ego's struggle without words. The voy-ager will usually not experience all of these states, but only one or some of them; or sometimes the return to reality can take completely new and unusual turns. In such a case the general instructions for the Third Bardo should be emphasized. (pp. 111ff).

I. General Description of the Third Bardo

Normally, the person descends, step by step, into lower (more con-stricted) states of consciousness. Each step downwards may be preceded by a swooning into unconsciousness. Occasionally the descent may be sudden, and the person will find himself jolted back to a vision of reality which by contrast with the preceding phases seems dull, static, hard, angular, ugly and puppet-like. Such changes can induce fear and horror and he may struggle desperately to regain familiar reality. He may get trapped into irrational or even bestial perspectives which then dominate his entire consciousness. These narrow primitive elements stem from aspects of his personal history which are usually repressed. The more enlightened consciousness of the first two Bardos and the civilized elements of ordinary waking life are shelved in favor of powerful, obsessive primitive impulses, which in fact are merely faded and incoherent instinctual parts of the voyager's total personality. The suggestibility of Bardo consciousness makes them seem all-powerful and overwhelming.

On the other hand, the voyager may also feel that he possesses supernormal powers of perception and movement, that he can perform miracles, extraordinary feats of bodily control, etc. The Tibetan book definitely attributes paranormal faculties to the consciousness of the Bardo voyager and explains it as due to the fact that the Bardo-consciousness encompasses future elements as well as past. Hence clairvoyance, telepathy, ESP, etc. are said to be possible. Objective evidence does not indicate whether this sense of increased perceptiveness is real or illusory. We therefore leave this as an open question, to be decided by empirical evidence.

This then is the *first* recognition point of the Third Bardo. The feeling of supernormal perception and performance. Assuming that it is valid, the manual warns the voyager not to be fascinated by his heightened powers, and not to exercise them. In yogic practice, the most advanced of the *lamas* teach the disciple not to strive after psychic powers of this nature for their own sake; for until the disciple is morally fit to use them wisely, they become a serious impediment to his higher spiritual development. Not until the selfish, game-involved nature of man is completely mastered is he safe in using them.

A *second* sign of Third Bardo existence are experiences of panic, torture and persecution. They are distinguished from the wrathful visions of the Second Bardo in that they definitely seem to involve the person's own "skin-encapsulated ego." Mind-controlling manipulative figures and demons of hideous aspects may be hallucinated. The form that these torturing demons take will depend on the person's cultural background. Where Tibetans saw demons and beasts of prey, a Westerner may see impersonal machinery grinding, or depersonalizing and controlling devices of different futuristic varieties. Visions of world destruction, dying in space-fiction modes, and hallucinations of being engulfed by destructive powers will likewise come; and sounds of the mind-controlling apparatus, of the "combine's fog machinery," of the gears which move the scenery of the puppet show, of angry overflowing seas, and of the roaring of fire and of fierce winds springing up, and of mocking laughter.

When these sounds and visions come, the first impulse will be to flee from them in panic and terror, not caring where one goes, so long as one goes out. In psychedelic drug experiences, the person may at this time plead or demand to be brought "out of it" through antidotes or tranquillizers. The person may see himself as about to fall down deep, terrifying precipices. These symbolize the so-called evil passions which, like narcotic drugs, enslave and bind mankind to existence in game-networks *(sangsāra):* anger, lust, stupidity, pride or egoism, jealousy, and control-power. Such experiences, just as the previous one of enhanced power, should be regarded as recognizing features of the Third Bardo. One should neither flee the pain nor pursue the pleasure. *Recognition is all that is necessary*—and recognition depends upon preparation.

A *third* sign is a kind of restless, unhappy wandering which may be purely mental or may involve actual physical movement. The person feels as if driven by winds (winds of *karma*) or shunted around mechanically. There may be brief respites at certain places or scenes in the "ordinary" human world. Like a person travelling alone at night along a highway, having his attention arrested by prominent landmarks, great isolated trees, houses, bridgeheads, temples, hot-dog stands, etc., the person in the re-entry period has similar experiences. He may demand to return to familiar haunts in the human world. But any such external placation is temporary and soon the restless wandering will recommence. There may come a desperate desire to phone or otherwise contact your family, your doctor, your friends and appeal to them to pull you out of the state. This desire should be resisted. The guide and the fellow voyagers can be of best assistance. One should not try to involve others in one's hallucinatory world. The attempt will fail anyway since outsiders are usually unable to understand what is happening. Again, merely to recognize these desires as Third Bardo manifestations is already the first step toward liberation.

A *fourth*, rather common experience is the following: the person may feel stupid and full of incoherent thoughts, whereas everyone else seems to be perfectly knowing and wise. This leads to feelings of guilt and inadequacy and in extreme form to the Judgment Vision, to be described below. This feeling of stupidity is merely the natural result of the limited perspective under which the consciousness is operating in this Bardo. Calm, relaxed acceptance and trust will enable the voyager to win liberation at this point.

Another experience, the *fifth* recognizing feature, which is especially impressive when it occurs suddenly, is the feeling of being dead, cut off from surrounding life, and full of misery. The person may with a jolt awake from some trance-like swoon and experience himself and the others as lifeless robots, performing wooden meaningless gestures. He may feel that he will never come back and will lament his miserable state.

Again, such fantasies are to be recognized as the attempts of the ego to regain control. In the true state of ego-death, as it occurs in the First or Second Bardos, such complaints are never uttered.

Sixth, one may have the feeling of being oppressed or crushed or squeezed into cracks and crevices amidst rocks and boulders. Or the person may feel that a kind of metallic net or cage may encompass him. This symbolizes the attempt prematurely to enter an ego-robot which is unfitting or unequipped to deal with the expanded consciousness. Therefore one should relax the panicky desire to regain an ego.

A *Seventh* aspect is a kind of grey twilight-like light suffusing everything, which is in marked contrast to the brilliantly radiating lights and colors of the earlier stages of the voyage. Objects, instead of shining, glowing and vibrating, are now dully colored, shabby and angular.

The passages on pages 111–14 contain general instructions for the Third Bardo state and its recognizable features. Any or all of the passages may be read when the guide senses that the voyager is beginning to return to the ego.

II. Re-entry Visions

In the preceding section the *symptoms* of re-entry were described, the signs that the voyager is trying to regain his ego. In this section are described visions of the types of re-entry one can make.

The Tibetan manual conceives of the voyager as returning eventually to one of six worlds of game existence *(sangsāra)*. That is, the re-entry to the ego can take place on one of six levels, or as one of six personality types. Two of these are higher than the normal human, three are lower. The highest, most illuminated, level is that of the *devas*, who are what Westerners would call saints, sages or divine teachers. They are the most enlightened people walking the earth. Gautama Buddha, Lao Tse, Christ. The second level is that of the *asuras*, who may be called titans or heroes, people with a more than human degree of power and vision. The third level is that of most normal human beings, struggling through game-networks, occasionally breaking free. The fourth level is that of primitive and animalistic incarnations. In this category we have the dog and the cock, symbolic of hypersexuality concomitant with jealousy; the pig, symbolizing lustful stupidity and uncleanliness; the industrious, hoarding ant; the insect or worm signifying an earthy or grovelling disposition; the snake, flashing in anger; the ape, full of rampaging primitive power; the snarling "wolf of the steppes;" the bird, soaring freely. Many more could be enumerated. In all cultures of the world people have adopted identities in the image of animals. In childhood and in dreams it is a process familiar to all. The fifth level is that of neurotics, frustrated lifeless spirits forever pursuing unsatisfied desires; the sixth and lowest level is hell or psychosis. Less than one percent of ego-transcendent experiences end in sainthood or psychosis. Most persons return to the normal human level.

According to the *Tibetan Book of the Dead*, each of the six game worlds or levels of existence is associated with a characteristic sort of thraldom, from which non-game experiences give temporary freedom: (1) existence as a *deva*, or saint, although more desirable than the others, is concomitant with an ever-recurring round of pleasure, free game ecstasy; (2) existence as an *asura*, or titan, is concomitant with incessant heroic warfare; (3) helplessness and slavery are characteristic of animal existence; (4) torments of unsatisfied needs and wants are characteristic of the existence of *pretas*, or unhappy spirits; (5) extremes of heat and cold, pleasure and pain, exist in hell; (6) the characteristic impediments of human existence are inertia, smug ignorance, physical or psychological handicaps of various sorts.

According to the *Bardo Thödol*, the level one is destined for is determined by one's *karma*. During the period of the Third Bardo premonitory signs and visions of the different levels appear, that for which one is heading appearing most clearly. For example, the voyager may feel full of godlike power *(asuras)*, or he may feel himself stirred by primitive or bestial impulses, or he may experience the all-pervasive frustration of the unhappy neurotics, or shudder at the tortures of a self-created hell.

The chances of making a favorable re-entry are increased if the process is allowed to take its own natural course, without effort or struggle. One should avoid pursuing or fleeing any of the visions, but meditate calmly on the knowledge that all levels exist in the Buddha also.

One can recognize and examine the signs as they appear and learn a great deal about oneself in a very short time. Although it is unwise to struggle against or flee the visions that come in this period, the instructions given (page 115) are designed to help the voyager regain First Bardo transcendence. In this way, if the person finds himself about to return to a personality or ego which he finds inappropriate to his new knowledge about himself, he can, by following the instructions, prevent this and make a fresh re-entry.

III. The All-Determining Influence of Thought

Liberation may be obtained, by such confrontation, even though previously it was not. If, however, liberation is not obtained even after these confrontations, further earnest and continued application is essential.

Should you feel attachment to material possessions, to old games and activities, or if you get angry because other people are still involved in pursuits that you have renounced, this will affect the psychological balance in such a way that even if destined to return at a higher level, you will actually re-enter on a lower level in the world of unsatisfied spirits (neurosis). On the other hand, even if you do feel attached to worldly games that you have renounced, you will not be able to play them, and they will be of no use to you. Therefore abandon weakness and attachment to them; cast them away wholly; renounce them from your heart. No matter who may be enjoying your possessions, or taking your role, have no feelings of miserliness or jealousy, but be prepared to renounce them willingly. Think that you are offering them to your internal freedom and to your expanded consciousness. Abide in the feeling of non-attachment, devoid of weakness and craving.

Again, when the activities of the other members of the session are wrong, careless, inattentive or distracting, when the agreement or contract is broken, and when purity of intention is lost by any participant, and frivolity and laxness take over (all of which can clearly be seen by the *Bardo* voyager) you may feel lack of faith and begin to doubt your beliefs. You will be able to perceive any anxiety or fear, any selfish actions, egocentric conduct and manipulative behavior. You may think: "Alas! they are playing me false, they have cheated and deceived." If you think thus, you will become extremely depressed, and through great resentment you will acquire disbelief and loss of faith, instead of affection and humble trust. Since this affects the psychological balance, re-entry will certainly be made on an unpleasant level.

Such thinking will not only be of no use, but it will do great harm. However improper the behavior of others, think thus: "What? How can the words of a Buddha be inappropriate? It is like the reflection of blemishes on my own face which I see in a mirror; my own thoughts must be impure. As for these others, they are noble in body, holy in speech, and the Buddha is within them: their actions are lessons for me."

Thus thinking, put your trust in your companions and exercise sincere love towards them. Then whatever they do will be to your benefit. The exercise of that love is very important; do not forget this!

Again, even if you were destined to return to a lower level and are already going into that existence, yet through the good deeds of friends, relatives, participants, learned teachers who devote themselves wholeheartedly to the correct performance of beneficent rituals, the delight from your feeling greatly cheered at seeing them will, by its own virtue, so affect the psychological balance that even though heading downwards, you may yet rise to a higher and happier level. Therefore you should not create selfish thoughts, but exercise pure affection and humble faith towards all, impartially. This is highly important. Hence be extremely careful.

The instructions given concerning the influence of thought (page 116) are useful in any phase of the Third Bardo, but particularly if the voyager is reacting with suspicion or resentment to other members of the group, or to his own friends and relatives.

IV. Judgment Visions

The judgment vision may come: the Third Bardo blame game. "Your good genius will count up your good deeds with white pebbles, the evil genius the evil deeds with black pebbles." A judgment scene is a central part of many religious systems, and the vision can assume various forms. Westerners are most likely to see it in the well-known Christian version. The Tibetans give a psychological interpretation to this as to all the other visions. The Judge, or Lord of Death, symbolizes conscience itself in its stern aspect of impartiality and love of righteousness. The "Mirror of Karma" (the Christian Judgment Book), consulted by the Judge, is memory. Different parts of the ego will come forward, some offering lame excuses to meet accusations, others ascribing baser motives to various deeds, counting apparently neutral deeds among the black ones; still others offering justifications or requests for pardon. The mirror of memory reflects clearly; lying and subterfuge will be of no avail. Be not frightened, tell no lies, face truth fearlessly.

Now you may imagine yourself surrounded by figures who wish to torment, torture or ridicule you (the "Executive Furies of the Robot Lord of Death"). These merciless figures may be internal or they may involve the people around you, seen as pitiless, mocking, superior. Remember that fear and guilt and persecuting, mocking figures are your own hallucinations. Your own guilt machine. Your personality is a collection of thought-patterns and void. It cannot be harmed or injured. "Swords cannot pierce it, fire cannot burn it." Free yourself from your own hallucinations. In reality there is no such thing as the Lord of Death, or a justice-dispensing god or demon or spirit. Act so as to recognize this.

Recognize that you are in the Third Bardo. Meditate upon your ideal symbol. If you do not know how to meditate, then merely analyze with great care the real nature of that which is frightening to you: "Reality" is nothing but a voidness (*Dharma-Kāya*). That voidness is not of the voidness of nothingness, but a voidness at the true nature of which you feel awed, and before which your consciousness shines more clearly and lucidly.*

*That is the state of mind known as *"Sambhoga-Kāya."* In that state, you experience, with unbearable intensity, Voidness and Brightness inseparable—the Voidness bright by nature

If the voyager is struggling with guilt and penance hallucinations, the instructions on page 117 may be read.

---

and the Brightness inseparable from the Voidness—a state of the primordial or unmodi-fied consciousness, which is the *Adi-Kayā*. And the power of this, shining unobstructedly, will radiate everywhere; it is the *Nirmāna-Kāya*.

These refer to the fundamental Wisdom Teachings of the *Bardo Thödol*. In all Tibetan systems of *yoga*, realization of the Voidness is the one great aim. To realize it is to attain the unconditioned Dharma-Kıya, or "Divine Body of Truth," the primordial state of un-createdness, of the supra-mundane All-Consciousness. The *Dharma-Kāya* is the highest of the three bodies of the Buddha and of all Buddhas and beings who have perfect en-lightenment. The other two bodies are the *Sambogha-Kāya* or "Divine Body of Perfect Endowment" and the *Nirmāna-Kāya* or "Divine Body of Incarnation." *Adi-Kāya* is syn-onymous with *Dharma-Kāya*. The *Dharma-Kāya* is primordial, formless Essential Wis-dom; it is true experience freed from all error or inherent or accidental obscuration. It includes both *Nirvāna* and *Sangsāra*, which are polar states of consciousness, but in the realm of pure consciousness identical. The *Sambhoga-Kāya* embodies, as in the five Dhyānī Buddhas, Reflected or Modified Wisdom; and the *Nirmāna-Kāya* embodies, as in the Human Buddhas, Practical or Incarnate Wisdom. All enlightened beings who are re-born in this or any other world with full consciousness, as workers for the betterment of their fellow creatures, are said to be *Nirmāna-Kāya* incarnates. Lama Kazi Dawa-Samdup, the translator of the *Bardo Thödol*, held that the *Adi-Buddha*, and all deities as-sociated with the *Dharma Kāya*, are not to be regarded as personal deities, but as personifications of primordial and universal forces, laws or spiritual influences. "In the boundless panorama of the existing and visible universe, whatever shapes appear, what-ever sounds vibrate, whatever radiances illuminate, or whatever consciousnesses cognize, all are the play or manifestation in the *Tri-Kāya*, the Three-fold Principle of the Cause of All Causes, the Primordial Trinity. Impenetrating all, is the All-Pervading Essence of Spirit, which is Mind. It is uncreated, impersonal, self-existing, immaterial and indestruc-tible." The *Tri-Kāya* is the esoteric trinity and corresponds to the exoteric trinity of the Buddha, the Scriptures and the Priesthood (or your own divinity, this manual and your companions).

V. Sexual Visions

Sexual visions are extremely frequent during the Third Bardo. You may see or imagine males and females copulating.* This vision may be internal or it may involve the people around you. You may hallucinate multi-person orgies and experience both desire and shame, attraction and disgust. You may wonder what sexual performance is expected of you and have doubts about your ability to perform at this time.

When these visions occur, remember to withhold yourself from action or attachment. Have faith and float gently with the stream. Trust in the unity of life and in your companions.

If you attempt to enter into your old ego because you are attracted or repulsed, if you try to join or escape from the orgy you are hallucinating, you will re-enter on an animal or neurotic level. If you become conscious of "maleness," hatred of the father together with jealousy and attraction towards the mother will be experienced; if you become conscious of "femaleness," hatred of the mother together with attraction and fondness for the father is experienced.

It is perhaps needless to say that this kind of self-centered sexuality has little in common with the sexuality of transpersonal experiences. Physical union can be one expression or manifestation of cosmic union.

Visions of sexual union may sometimes be followed by visions of conception—you may actually visualize the sperm uniting with the ovum—, of intra-uterine life and of birth through a womb. Some people claim to have re-lived their own physical birth in psychedelic sessions and occasionally confirming evidence for such claims has been put forward. Whether this is so or not may be left as a question to be decided by empirical evidence. Sometimes the birth visions will be

*According to Jung, ("Psychological Commentary" to the *Tibetan Book of the Dead*, Evans-Wentz edition, p. xiii), "Freud's theory is the first attempt made in the West to investigate, as if from below, from the animal sphere of instinct the psychic territory that corresponds in Tantric *Lamaism* to the *Sidpa Bardo*." The vision described here, in which the person sees mother and father in sexual intercourse, corresponds to the "primal scene" in psychoanalysis. At this level, then, we begin to see remarkable convergence of Eastern and Western psychology. Note also the exact correspondence to the psychoanalytic theory of the Oedipus Complex.

clearly symbolic—e.g., emergence from a cocoon, breaking out of a shell, etc.

Whether the birth vision is constructed from memory or fantasy, the psychedelic voyager should try to recognize the signs indicating the type of personality that is being reborn.

The appropriate instructions (page 119) may be read to the voyager who is struggling with sexual hallucinations.

VI. Methods for Preventing the Re-Entry

Although many confrontations and recognition points have been given, the person may be ill-prepared and still be wandering back to game reality. It is of advantage to postpone the return for as long as possible, thus maximizing the degree of enlightenment in the subsequent personality. For this reason four meditative methods are given for prolonging the ego-loss state. They are (1) meditation on the Buddha or guide (page 120); (2) concentration on good games (page 121); (3) meditation on illusion (page 122); and (4) meditation on the void (page 123). Each one attempts to lead the voyager back to the First Bardo central stream of energy from which he has been separated by game involvements. One may ask how these meditative methods, which seem difficult for the ordinary person, can be effective. The answer given in the Tibetan *Bardo Thödol* is that due to the increased suggestibility and openness of the mind in the psychedelic state these methods can be used by anyone, regardless of intellectual capacity, or proficiency in meditation.

VII. Methods of Choosing the Post-Session Personality

Choosing the post-session ego is an extremely profound art and should not be undertaken carelessly or hastily. One should *not* return fleeing from hallucinated tormentors. Such re-entry will tend to bring the person to one of the three lower levels. One should first banish the fear by visualizing one's protective figure or the Buddha; then choose calmly and impartially.

The limited foreknowledge available to the voyager should be used to make a wise choice. In the Tibetan tradition each of the levels of game-existence is associated with a particular color and also certain geographical symbols. These may be different for twentieth-century Westerners. Each person has to learn to decode his own internal road map. The Tibetan indicators may be used as a starting point. The purpose is clear: one should follow the signs of the three higher types and shun those of the three lower. One should follow light and pleasant visions and shun dark and dreary ones.

The world of saints *(devas)* is said to shine with a white light and to be preceded by visions of delightful temples and jewelled mansions. The world of heroes *(asuras)* has a green light and is signalled by magical forests and fire images. The ordinary human world has a yellow light. Animal existence is foreshadowed by a blue light and images of caves and deep holes in the earth. The world of neurotics or unsatisfied spirits has a red light and visions of desolate plains and forest wastes. The hell world emits a smoke-colored light and is preceded by sounds of wailing, visions of gloomy lands, black and white houses and black roads along which you have to travel.

Use your foresight to choose a good post-session robot. Do not be attracted to your old ego. Whether you choose to pursue power, or status, or wisdom, or learning, or servitude, or whatever, choose impartially, without being attracted or repelled. Enter into game existence with good grace, voluntarily and freely. Visualize it as a celestial mansion, i.e., as an opportunity to exercise game-ecstasy. Have faith in the protection of the deities and choose. The mood of complete impartiality is important since you may be in error. A game that appears good may later turn out to be bad. Complete impartiality, freedom from want or fear, ensure that a maximally wise choice is made.

As you return you see spread out before you the world, your former life, a planet full of fascinating objects and events. Each aspect of the return trip can be a delightful discovery. Soon you will be descending to take your place in worldly events. The key to this return voyage is simply this: take it easy, slowly, naturally. Enjoy every second. Don't rush. Don't be attached to your old games. Recognize that you are in the re-entry period. Do not return with any emotional pressure. Everything you see and touch can glow with radiance. Each moment can be a joyous discovery.

Here ends the Third Bardo,
the Period of Re-Entry

General Conclusion

Well-prepared students with advanced spiritual understanding can use the "Transference" principle at the moment of ego-death and need not traverse subsequent Bardo states. They will rise to a state of illumination and remain there throughout the entire period. Others, who are a little less experienced in spiritual discipline, will recognize the Clear Light in the second stage of the First Bardo and will then win liberation. Others, at a still less advanced level, may be liberated while experiencing one of the positive or negative visions of the Second Bardo. Since there are several turning points, liberation can be obtained at one or the other through recognition at moments of confrontation. Those of very weak *karmic* connection, i.e., those who have been involved in heavy ego-dominated game-playing, will have to wander downwards to the Third Bardo. Again, many points for liberation have been charted. The weakest persons will fall under the influence of guilt and terror. For weaker persons there are various graded teachings for preventing the return to routine-reality, or at least for choosing it wisely. Through applying the methods of visualization described, they should be able to experience the benefits of the session. Even those persons whose familiar routines are primitive and egocentric can be prevented from entering into misery. Once they have experienced, for however short a period, the great beauty and power of a free awareness, they may, in the next period, meet with a guide or friend who will initiate them further into the way.

The way in which this teaching is effective, even for a voyager already in the *Sidpa Bardo*, is as follows: each person has some positive and some negative game-residues *(karma)*. The continuity of consciousness has been broken by an ego-death for which the person was not prepared. The teachings are like a trough in a broken water drain, temporarily restoring the continuity with positive *karma*. As stated before, the extreme suggestibility or detached quality of consciousness in this state ensures the efficacy of listening to the doctrine. The teaching embedded in this Manual may be compared to a catapult which can direct the person towards the goal of liberation. Or like the moving of a big wooden beam, which is so heavy that a hundred men cannot carry it, but by being floated on water it can be easily moved. Or it is like controlling a horse's bit and course by the use of a bridle.

Therefore, these teachings should be vividly impressed on the voyager, again and again. This Manual may also be used more generally. It should be recited as often as possible and committed to memory as far as possible. When ego-death or final death comes, recognize the symptoms, recite the Manual to yourself, and reflect upon the meaning. If you cannot do it yourself, ask a friend to read it for you. There is no doubt as to its liberative power.

It liberates by being seen or heard, without need of ritual or complex meditation. This Profound Teaching liberates those of great evil *karma* through the Secret Pathway. One should not forget its meaning and the words, even though pursued by seven mastiffs. By this Select Teaching, one obtains Buddhahood at the moment of ego-loss. Were the Buddhas of past, present and future to seek, they could not find any doctrine transcending this.

Here ends the Bardo Thödol, known as
The Tibetan Book of the Dead

III.
SOME TECHNICAL COMMENTS ABOUT PSYCHEDELIC SESSIONS

Use of This Manual

The most important use of this manual is for preparatory reading. Having read the Tibetan Manual, one can immediately recognize symptoms and experiences which might otherwise be terrifying, only because of lack of understanding as to what was happening. *Recognition* is the key word.

Secondly, this guidebook may be used to avoid paranoid traps or to regain the First Bardo transcendence if it has been lost. If the experience starts with light, peace, mystic unity, understanding, and if it continues along this path, then there is no need to remember this manual or have this manual re-read to you. Like a road map, we consult it only when lost, or when we wish to change course. Usually, however, the ego clings to its old games. There may be momentary discomfort or confusion. If this happens, the others present should not be sympathetic or show alarm. They should be prepared to stay calm and restrain their "helping games." In particular, the "doctor" role should be avoided.

If at any time you find yourself struggling to get back to routine reality, you can (by pre-arrangement) have a more experienced person, a fellow-voyager, or a trusted observer read parts of this manual to you.

Passages suitable for reading during the session are given in Part IV below. Each major descriptive section of the Tibetan Book has an appropriate instruction text. One may want to pre-record selected passages and simply flick on the recorder when desired. The aim of these instruction texts is always to lead the voyager back to the original First Bardo transcendence and to help maintain that as long as possible.

A third use would be to construct a "program" for a session using passages from the text. The aim would be to lead the voyager to one of the visions deliberately, or through a sequence of visions. The guide or friend could read the relevant passages, show slides or pictures of symbolic figures of processes, play carefully selected music, etc. One can envision a high art or programming psychedelic sessions, in which symbolic manipulations and presentations would lead the voyager through ecstatic visionary Bead Games.

Planning a Session

In planning a session, the first question to be decided is "what is the goal?" Classic Hinduism suggests four possibilities:

1. For increased personal power, intellectual understanding, sharpened insight into self and culture, improvement of life situation, accelerated learning, professional growth.
2. For duty, help of others, providing care, rehabilitation, rebirth for fellow men.
3. For fun, sensuous enjoyment, aesthetic pleasure, interpersonal closeness, pure experience.
4. For transcendence, liberation from ego and space-time limits; attainment of mystical union.

This manual aims primarily at the latter goal—that of liberation-enlightenment. This emphasis does not preclude attainment of the other goals—in fact, it guarantees their attainment because illumination requires that the person be able to step out beyond game problems of personality, role, and professional status. The initiate can decide beforehand to devote the psychedelic experience to any of the four goals. The manual will be of assistance in any event.

If there are several people having a session together they should either agree collaboratively on a goal, or at least be aware of each other's goals. If the session is to be "programmed" then the participants should either agree on or design a program collaboratively, or they should agree to let one member of the group do the programming. Unexpected or undesired manipulations by one of the participants can easily "trap" the other voyagers into paranoid Third Bardo delusions.

The voyager, especially in an individual session, may also wish to have either an extroverted or an introverted experience. In the *extroverted* transcendent experience, the self is ecstatically fused with external objects (e.g. flowers, or other people). In the *introverted* state, the self is ecstatically fused with internal life processes (lights, energy-waves, bodily events, biological forms, etc.). Of course, either the extroverted or the introverted state may be negative rather than positive, depending on the attitude of the voyager. Also it may be primarily conceptual or primarily emotional. The eight types of experience thus derived (four positive and four negative) have been described more fully in Visions 2 to 5 of the Second Bardo.

For the extroverted mystic experience one would bring to the session objects or symbols to guide the awareness in the desired direction. Candles, pictures, books, incense, music or recorded passages. An introverted mystic experience requires the elimination of all stimulation; no light, no sound, no smell, no movement.

The *mode of communication* with the other participants should also be agreed on beforehand. You may agree on certain signals, silently indicating companionship. You may arrange for physical contact—clasping hands, embracing. These means of communication should be pre-arranged to avoid game-misinterpretations that may develop during the heightened sensitivity of ego-transcendence.

Drugs and Dosages

A wide variety of chemicals and plants have psychedelic ("mind-manifesting") effects. The most widely used substances are listed here together with dosages adequate for a normal adult of average size. The dosage to be taken depends, of course, on the goal of the session. Two figures are therefore given. The first column indicates a dosage which should be sufficient for an inexperienced person to enter the transcendental worlds described in this manual. The second column gives a smaller dosage figure, which may be used by more experienced persons or by participants in a group session.

	A	B
LSD-25 (lysergic acid diethylamide)	200–500 μg	100–200 μg
Mescaline	600–800 mg	300–500 mg
Psilocybin	40–60 mg	20–30 mg

The time of onset, when the drugs are taken orally on an empty stomach, is approximately 20–30 minutes for LSD and psilocybin, and one to two hours for mescaline. The duration of the session is usually eight to ten hours for LSD and mescaline, and five to six hours for psilocybin. DMT (dimethyltryptamine), when injected intramuscularly in dosages of 50–60 mg, gives an experience approximately equivalent to 500 μg of LSD, but which lasts only 30 minutes.

Some persons have found it useful to take other drugs before the session. A very anxious person, for example, may take 30 to 40 mg of Librium about one hour earlier, to calm and relax himself. Methedrine has also been used to induce a pleasant, euphoric mood prior to the session. Sometimes, with excessively nervous persons, it is advisable to stagger the drug-administration: for example, 200 μg of LSD may be taken initially, and a "booster" of another 200 μg may be taken after the person has become familiar with some of the effects of the psychedelic state.

Nausea may sometimes occur. Usually this is a mental symptom, indicating fear, and should be regarded as such. Sometimes, however, particularly with the use of morning-glory seeds and peyote, the nausea can have a physiological cause. Anti-nauseant drugs such as

Marezine, Bonamine, Dramamine or Tigan, may be taken beforehand to prevent this.

If a person becomes trapped in a repetitive game-routine during a session, it is sometimes possible to "break the set" by administering 50 mg of DMT, or even 25 mg of Dexedrine or Methedrine. Such additional dosages, of course, should only be given with the person's own knowledge and consent.

Should external emergencies call for it, Thorazine (100–200 mg, i.m.) or other phenothiazine-type tranquilizers will terminate the effects of psychedelic drugs. Antidotes should not be used simply because the voyager or the guide is frightened. Instead, the appropriate sections of the Third Bardo should be read.*

---

*Further, more detailed suggestions concerning dosage may be found in a paper by Gary M. Fisher: "Some Comments Concerning Dosage Levels of Psychedelic Compounds for Psychotherapeutic Experiences." *Psychedelic Review, I*, no. 2, pp. 208–218, 1963.

Preparation

Psychedelic chemicals are not drugs in the usual sense of the word. There is no specific reaction, no expected sequence of events, somatic or psychological.

The specific reaction has little to do with the chemical and is chiefly a function of *set* and *setting*; preparation and environment. The better the preparation, the more ecstatic and revelatory the session. In initial sessions and with unprepared persons, setting—particularly the actions of others—is most important. With persons who have prepared thoughtfully and seriously, the setting is less important.

There are two aspects of set: long-range and immediate.

Long-range set refers to the personal history, the enduring personality. The kind of person you are—your fears, desires, conflicts, guilts, secret passions—determines how you interpret and manage any situation you enter, including a psychedelic session. Perhaps more important are the reflex mechanisms used when dealing with anxiety—the defenses, the protective maneuvers typically employed. Flexibility, basic trust, religious faith, human openness, courage, interpersonal warmth, creativity, are characteristics which allow for fun and easy learning. Rigidity, desire to control, distrust, cynicism, narrowness, cowardice, coldness, are characteristics which make any new situation threatening. Most important is insight. No matter how many cracks in the record, the person who has some understanding of his own recording machinery, who can recognize when he is not functioning as he would wish, is better able to adapt to any challenge—even the sudden collapse of his ego.

The most careful preparation would include some discussion of the personality characteristics and some planning with the guide as to how to handle expected emotional reactions when they occur.

Immediate set refers to the expectations about the session itself. Session preparation is of critical importance in determining how the experience unfolds. People tend naturally to impose their personal and social game perspectives on any new situation. Careful thought should precede the session to prevent narrow sets being imposed.

Medical expectations. Some ill-prepared subjects unconsciously impose a medical model on the experience. They look for symptoms, interpret each new sensation in terms of sickness or health, place the guide in a doctor-role, and, if anxiety develops, demand chemical rebirth — i.e., tranquillizers. Occasionally one hears of casual, ill-planned, non-guided sessions which end in the subject demanding to be hospitalized, etc. It is even more problem-provoking if the guide employs a medical model, watches for symptoms, and keeps hospitalization in mind to fall back on, as protection for himself.

Rebellion against convention may be the motive of some people who take the drug. The idea of doing something "far out" or vaguely naughty is a naive set which can color the experience.

Intellectual expectations are appropriate when subjects have had much psychedelic experience. Indeed, LSD offers vast possibilities for accelerated learning and scientific-scholarly research. But for initial sessions, intellectual reactions can become traps. The Tibetan Manual never tires of warning about the dangers of rationalization. "Turn your mind off" is the best advice for novitiates. Control of your consciousness is like flight instruction. After you have learned how to move your consciousness around — into ego-loss and back, at will — then intellectual exercises can be incorporated into the psychedelic experience. The last stage of the session is the best time to examine concepts. The objective of this particular manual is to free you from your verbal mind for as long as possible.

Religious expectations invite the same advice as intellectual set. Again, the subject in early sessions is best advised to float with the stream, stay "up" as long as possible, and postpone theological interpretations until the end of the session, or to later sessions.

Recreational and aesthetic expectations are natural. The psychedelic experience, without question, provides ecstatic moments which dwarf any personal or cultural game. Pure sensation can capture awareness. Interpersonal intimacy reaches Himalayan heights. Aesthetic delights — musical, artistic, botanical, natural — are raised to the millionth power. But all these reactions can be Third Bardo ego games: "*I* am having this ecstasy. How lucky *I* am!" Such reactions can become tender traps, preventing the subject from reaching pure ego-loss (First Bardo) or the glories of Second Bardo creativity.

Planned expectations. This manual prepares the person for a mystical experience according to the Tibetan model. The Sages of the Snowy Ranges have developed a most sophisticated and precise understanding of human psychology, and the student who studies this manual will become oriented for a voyage which is much richer in scope and meaning than any Western psychological theory. We remain aware, however, that the *Bardo Thödol* model of consciousness is a human artifact, a Second Bardo hallucination, however grand its scope.

Some practical recommendations. The subject should set aside at least three days for his experience; a day before, the session day, and a follow-up day. This scheduling guarantees a reduction in external pressure and a more sober commitment to the voyage.

Talking to others who have taken the voyage is excellent preparation, although the Second Bardo hallucinatory quality of all descriptions should be recognized. Observing a session is another valuable preliminary. The opportunity to see others during and after a session shapes expectations.

Reading books about mystical experience is a standard orientation procedure. Reading the accounts of others' experiences is another possibility (Aldous Huxley, Alan Watts, and Gordon Wasson have written powerful accounts).

Meditation is probably the best preparation for a psychedelic session. Those who have spent time in the solitary attempt to manage the mind, to eliminate thought and to reach higher stages of concentration, are the best candidates for a psychedelic session. When the ego-loss state occurs, they are ready. They recognize the process as an end eagerly awaited, rather than a strange event ill-understood.

The Setting

The first and most important thing to remember, in the preparation for a psychedelic session, is to provide a setting which is removed from one's usual social and interpersonal games and which is as free as possible from unforeseen distractions and intrusions. The voyager should make sure that he will not be disturbed by visitors or telephone calls, since these will often jar him into hallucinatory activity. Trust in the surroundings and privacy are necessary.

A period of time (usually at least three days) should be set aside in which the experience will run its natural course and there will be sufficient time for reflection and meditation. It is important to keep schedules open for three days and to make these arrangements beforehand. A too-hasty return to game-involvements will blur the clarity of the vision and reduce the potential for learning. If the experience was with a group, it is very useful to stay together after the session in order to share and exchange experiences.

There are differences between night sessions and day sessions. Many people report that they are more comfortable in the evening and consequently that their experiences are deeper and richer. The person should choose the time of day that seems right according to his own temperament at first. Later, he may wish to experience the difference between night and day sessions.

Similarly, there are differences between sessions out-of-doors and indoors. Natural settings such as gardens, beaches, forests, and open country have specific influences which one may or may not wish to incur. The essential thing is to feel as comfortable as possible in the surroundings, whether in one's living room or under the night sky. A familiarity with the surroundings may help one to feel confident in hallucinatory periods. If the session is held indoors, one must consider the arrangement of the room and the specific objects one may wish to see and hear during the experience.

Music, lighting, the availability of food and drink, should be considered beforehand. Most people report no desire for food during the height of the experience, and then, later on, prefer to have simple, ancient foods like bread, cheese, wine, and fresh fruit. Hunger is usually not the issue. The senses are wide open, and the taste and smell of a fresh orange are unforgettable.

In group sessions, the arrangement of the room is quite important. People usually will not feel like walking or moving very much for a long period, and either beds or mattresses should be provided. The arrangement of the beds or mattresses can vary. One suggestion is to place the heads of the beds together to form a star pattern. Perhaps one may want to place a few beds together and keep one or two some distance apart for anyone who wishes to remain aside for some time. Often, the availability of an extra room is desirable for someone who wishes to be in seclusion for a period.

If it is desired to listen to music or to reflect on paintings or religious objects, one should arrange these so that everyone in the group feels comfortable with what they are hearing or seeing. In a group session, all decisions about goals, setting, etc. should be made with collaboration and openness.

The Psychedelic Guide

For initial sessions, the attitude and behavior of the guide are critical factors. He possesses enormous power to shape the experience. With the cognitive mind suspended, the subject is in a heightened state of suggestibility. The guide can move consciousness with the slightest gesture or reaction.

The key issue here is the guide's ability to turn off his own ego and social games—in particular, to muffle his own power needs and his fears. To be there relaxed, solid, accepting, secure. The Tao wisdom of creative quietism. To sense all and do nothing except to let the subject know your wise presence.

A psychedelic session lasts up to twelve hours and produces moments of intense, *intense*, INTENSE reactivity. The guide must never be bored, talkative, intellectualizing. He must remain calm during long periods of swirling mindlessness.

He is the ground control in the airport tower. Always there to receive messages and queries from high-flying aircraft. Always ready to help navigate their course, to help them reach their destination. An airport-tower-operator who imposes his own personality, his own games upon the pilot is unheard of. The pilots have their own flight plan, their own goals, and ground control is there, ever waiting to be of service.

The pilot is reassured to know that an expert who has guided thousands of flights is down there, available for help. But suppose the flier has reason to suspect that ground control is harboring his own motives and might be manipulating the plane towards selfish goals. The bond of security and confidence would crumble.

It goes without saying, then, that the guide should have had considerable experience in psychedelic sessions himself and in guiding others. To administer psychedelics without personal experience is unethical and dangerous.

The greatest problem faced by human beings in general, and the psychedelic guide in particular, is *fear*. Fear of the unknown. Fear of losing control. Fear of trusting the genetic process and your companions. From our own research studies and our investigations into sessions run by others—serious professionals or adventurous bohemians—we have been led to the conclusion that almost every negative LSD reaction has been caused by fear on the part of the guide which has augmented the transient fear of the subject. When the guide acts to protect himself, he communicates his concern to the subject.

The guide must remain passively sensitive and intuitively relaxed for several hours. This is a difficult assignment for most Westerners. For this reason, we have sought ways to assist the guide in maintaining a state of alert quietism in which he is poised with ready flexibility. The most certain way to achieve this state is for the guide to take a low dose of the psychedelic with the subject. Routine procedure is to have one trained person participate in the experience and one staff member present in ground control without psychedelic aid.

The knowledge that one experienced guide is "up" and keeping the subject company, is of inestimable value; intimacy and communication; cosmic companionship; the security of having a trained pilot flying at your wing tip; the scuba diver's security in the presence of an expert comrade in the deep.

It is not recommended that guides take large doses during sessions for new subjects. The less experienced he is, the more likely will the subject impose Second and Third Bardo hallucinations. These intense games affect the experienced guide, who is likely to be in a state of mindless void. The guide is then pulled into the hallucinatory field of the subject, and may have difficulty orienting himself. During the First Bardo there are no familiar fixed landmarks, no place to put your foot, no solid concept upon which to base your thinking. All is flux. Decisive Second Bardo action on the part of the subject can structure the guide's flow if he has taken a heavy dose.

The role of the psychedelic guide is perhaps the most exciting and inspiring role in society. He is literally a liberator, one who provides illumination, one who frees men from their life-long internal bondage. To be present at the moment of awakening, to share the ecstatic revelation when the voyager discovers the wonder and awe of the divine life-process, is for many the most gratifying part to play in the evolutionary drama. The role of the psychedelic guide has a built-in protection against professionalism and didactic oneupmanship. The psychedelic liberation is so powerful that it far outstrips earthly game ambitions. Awe and gratitude—rather than pride—are the rewards of this new profession.

Composition of the Group

The most effective use of this manual will be for the experience of one person with a guide. However, the manual will be useful in a group also. When used in a group session, the following suggestions will be most helpful in planning.

The important thing to remember in organizing a group session is to have knowledge of and trust in the fellow voyagers. Trust in oneself and in one's companions is essential. If preparing for an experience with strangers, it is very important to share as much time and space as possible with them prior to the session. The participants should set collaborative goals and explore mutually their expectations and feelings and past experiences.

The size of the group should depend to some extent on how much experience the participants have had. Initially, small groups are preferable to larger ones. In any case, group experiences exceeding six or seven people are demonstrably less profound and generate more paranoid hallucinations. If planning for a group session of five or six people, it is preferable to have at least two guides present. One will take the psychedelic substance and the other, who does not, serves as a practical guide to take care of such concerns as changing the recordings, providing food, etc., and if necessary or desired, reading selections from the manual. If it is possible, one of the guides should be an experienced woman who can provide an atmosphere of spiritual nurturing and comfort.

It is sometimes advisable that the initial session of married couples be separate in order that the exploration of their marriage game not dominate the session. With some experience in consciousness-expansion, the marriage game like others may be explored for any purpose—increased intimacy, clearer communication, exploration of the foundations of the sexual, mating relationship, etc.

Follow-up

Just as one day should be set aside for preparation, so also should at least one day (preferably more) be reserved for follow-up. Game schedules should be minimal, and no routine appointments or commitments made. A transcendent experience can be soul-shaking, and it is often painful to return at once to game reality. The person should avoid thinking too much about the session at first. His brain is like a computer that has received a huge amount of new information to be assimilated. Attempts to rationalize, explain, understand intellectually, are usually made prematurely, sometimes even during the session. This is to be avoided. Maximal benefit accrues if the brain-computer is given ample time without pressure to work through and integrate the vast quantities of new impressions. Thus, the first rule for the follow-up period is: avoid too much thinking and talking. Rest, relax, avoid games.

Sometime toward the end of the post-session day, the voyager should meet with the guide or fellow voyagers to give a verbal account of his experience. Some of the most revealing insights can come from these comparisons. Each person has shot his own film, and the discrepancies and similarities between the different versions of the same behavioral or external events can yield startling clarifications.

IV.
INSTRUCTIONS FOR USE DURING A PSYCHEDELIC SESSION

First Bardo Instructions

O *(name of voyager)*
The time has come for you to seek new levels of reality.
Your ego and the *(name)* game are about to cease.
You are about to be set face to face with the Clear Light.
You are about to experience it in its reality.
In the ego-free state, wherein all things are like the void and
    cloudless sky,
And the naked spotless intellect is like a transparent vacuum;
At this moment, know yourself and abide in that state.

O *(name of voyager)*,
That which is called ego-death is coming to you.
Remember:
This is now the hour of death and rebirth;
Take advantage of this temporary death to obtain the perfect state—
Enlightenment.
Concentrate on the unity of all living beings.
Hold onto the Clear Light.
Use it to attain understanding and love.
If you cannot maintain the bliss of illumination and if you are
    slipping back into contact with the external world,
Remember:
The hallucinations which you may now experience,
The visions and insights,
Will teach you much about yourself and the world.
The veil of routine perception will be torn from your eyes.
Remember the unity of all living things.
Remember the bliss of the Clear Light.
Let it guide you through the visions of this experience.
Let it guide you through your new life to come.
If you feel confused; call upon the memory of your friends and the
    power of the person whom you most admire.

O *(name)*,
Try to reach and keep the experience of the Clear Light.

Remember:
The light is the life energy.
The endless flame of life.
An ever-changing surging turmoil of color may engulf your vision.
This is the ceaseless transformation of energy.
The life process.
Do not fear it.
Surrender to it.
Join it.
It is part of you.
You are part of it.
Remember also:
Beyond the restless flowing electricity of life is the ultimate reality—
The Void.
Your own awareness, not formed into anything possessing form or
    color, is naturally void.
The Final Reality.
The All Good.
The All Peaceful.
The Light.
The Radiance.
The movement is the fire of life from which we all come.
Join it.
It is part of you.
Beyond the light of life is the peaceful silence of the void.
The quiet bliss beyond all transformations.
The Buddha smile.
The Void is not nothingness.
The Void is beginning and end itself.
Unobstructed; shining, thrilling, blissful.
Diamond consciousness.
The All-Good Buddha.
Your own consciousness, not formed into anything,
No thought, no vision, no color, is void.
The intellect shining and blissful and silent—
This is the state of perfect enlightenment.

Your own consciousness, shining, void and inseparable from the
    great body of radiance, has no birth, nor death.
It is the immutable light which the Tibetans call Buddha Amitabha,
The awareness of the formless beginning.
Knowing this is enough.
Recognize the voidness of your own consciousness to be
    Buddhahood.
Keep this recognition and you will maintain the state of the divine
    mind of the Buddha.

Second Bardo Preliminary Instructions

Remember:
In this session you experience three Bardos,
Three states of ego-loss.
First there is the Clear Light of Reality.
Next there are fantastically varied game hallucinations.
Later you will reach the stage of Re-Entry
Of regaining an ego.

O friend,
You may experience ego-transcendence,
Departure from your old self.
But you are not the only one.
It comes to all at some time.
You are fortunate to have this gratuitously given rebirth experience.
Do not cling in fondness and weakness to your old self.
Even though you cling to your mind, you have lost the power to keep
　　it.
You can gain nothing by struggling in this hallucinatory world.
Be not attached.
Be not weak.
Whatever fear or terror may come to you
Forget not these words.
Take their meaning into your heart.
Go forward.
Herein lies the vital secret of recognition.

O friend, remember:
When body and mind separate, you experience a glimpse of the pure
　　truth—
Subtle, sparkling, bright,
Dazzling, glorious, and radiantly awesome,
In appearance like a mirage moving across a landscape in springtime.
One continuous stream of vibrations.
Be not daunted thereby,
Nor terrified, nor awed.

That is the radiance of your own true nature.
Recognize it.

From the midst of that radiance
Comes the natural sound of reality,
Reverberating like a thousand thunders simultaneously sounding.
That is the natural sound of your own life process.
Be not daunted thereby,
Nor terrified, nor awed.
It is sufficient for you to know that these apparitions are your own
    thought-forms.
If you do not recognize your own thought forms,
If you forget your preparation,
The lights will daunt you,
The sounds will awe you,
The rays will terrify you,
The people around you will confuse you.
Remember the key to the teachings.

O friend,
These realms are not come from somewhere ouside your self,
They come from within and shine upon you.
The revelations too are not come from somewhere else;
They exist from eternity within the faculties of your own intellect.
Know them to be of that nature.
The key to enlightenment and serenity during the period of ten
    thousand visions is simply this:
Relax.
Merge yourself with them.
Blissfully accept the wonders of your own creativity.
Become neither attached nor afraid,
Neither be attracted nor repulsed.
Above all, *do nothing* about the visions.
They exist only within you.

Instructions for Vision 1: The Source
(Eyes closed, external stimuli ignored)

O nobly-born, listen carefully:
The Radiant Energy of the Seed
From which come all living forms,
Shoots forth and strikes against you
With a light so brilliant that you will scarcely be able to look at it.
Do not be frightened.
This is the Source Energy which has been radiating for billions of
    years,
Ever manifesting itself in different forms.
Accept it.
Do not try to intellectualize it.
Do not play games with it.
Merge with it.
Let it flow through you.
Lose yourself in it.
Fuse in the Halo of Rainbow Light
Into the core of the energy dance.
Obtain Buddhahood in the Central Realm of the Densely Packed.

Instructions for Physical Symptoms

O friend, listen carefully.

The bodily symptoms you are having are not drug-effects.

They indicate that you are struggling against the awareness of
feelings which surpass your normal experience.

You cannot control these universal energy-waves.

Let the feelings melt all over you.

Become part of them.

Sink into them and through them.

Allow yourself to pulsate with the vibrations surrounding you.

Relax.

Do not struggle.

Your symptoms will disappear as soon as all trace of ego-centered
striving disappears.

Accept them as the message of the body.

Welcome them. Enjoy them.

Instructions for Vision 2:
The Internal Flow of Archetypal Processes
(Eyes closed, external stimuli ignored; intellectual aspects)

O nobly born, listen carefully:
The life flow is whirling through you.
An endless parade of pure forms and sounds,
Dazzlingly brilliant,
Ever-changing.
Do not try to control it.
Flow with it.
Experience the ancient cosmic myths of creation and manifestation.
Do not try to understand;
There is plenty of time for that later.
Merge with it.
Let it flow through you.
There is no need to act or think.
You are being taught the great lessons of evolution, creation,
    reproduction.
If you try to stop it, you may fall into hell-worlds and endure
    unbearable misery generated by your own mind.
Avoid game interpretations.
Avoid thinking, talking or doing.
Keep faith in the life flow.
Trust your companions on this watery journey.
Merge in Rainbow Light,
Into the Heart of The River of Created Forms.
Obtain Buddhahood in the Realm called Pre-Eminently Happy.

Instructions for Vision 3:
The Fire-Flow of Internal Unity
(Eyes closed, external stimuli ignored, emotional aspects)

O nobly born, listen carefully:
You are flowing outward into the fluid unity of life.
The ecstasy of organic fire glows in every cell.
The hard, dry, brittle husks of your ego are washing out,
Washing out to the endless sea of creation.
Flow with it.
Feel the pulse of the sun's heart.
Let the red Buddha *Amitabha* sweep you along.
Do not fear the ecstasy.
Do not resist the flow.
Remember, all the exultant power comes from within.
Release your attachment.
Recognize the wisdom of your own blood.
Trust the tide-force pulling you into unity with all living forms.
Let your heart burst in love for all life.
Let your warm blood gush out into the ocean of all life.
Do not be attached to the ecstatic power;
It comes from you.
Let it flow.
Do not try to hold on to your old bodily fears.
Let your body merge with the warm flux.
Let your roots sink into the warm life body.
Merge into the Heart-Glow of the Buddha *Amitabha*.
Float in the Rainbow Sea.
Attain Buddhahood in the Realm named Exultant Love.

Instructions for Vision 4:
The Wave-Vibration Structure of External Forms
(Eyes open, rapt involvement with external visual stimuli,
intellectual aspects)

O nobly born, listen carefully:
At this point you can become aware of the wave structure of the
    world around you.
Everything you see dissolves into energy vibrations.
Look closely and you will tune in on the electric dance of energy.
There are no longer things and persons but only the direct flow of
    particles.
Consciousness will now leave your body and flow into the stream of
    wave rhythm.
There is no need for talk or action.
Let your brain become a receiving set for the radiance.
All interpretations are the products of your own mind.
Dispel them. Have no fear.
Exult in the natural power of your own brain,
The wisdom of your own electricity.
Abide in the state of quietude.
As the three-dimensional world fragments, you may feel panic;
You may beget a fondness for the heavy dull world of objects you are
    leaving.
At this time, fear not the transparent, radiant, dazzling wave energy.
Allow your intellect to rest.
Fear not the hook-rays of the light of life,
The basic structure of matter,
The basic form of wave communication.
Watch quietly and receive the message.
You will now experience directly the revelation of primal forms.

Instructions for Vision 5:
The Vibratory Waves of External Unity
(Eyes open; rapt involvement with external stimuli such as lights, or
movements; emotional aspects)

O nobly born, listen carefully:
You are experiencing the unity of all living forms.
If people seem to you rubbery and lifeless, like plastic puppets,
Be not afraid.
This is only the attempt of the ego to maintain its separate identity.
Allow yourself to feel the unity of all.
Merge with the world around you.
Be not afraid.
Enjoy the dance of the puppets.
They are created by your own mind.
Allow yourself to relax and feel the ecstatic energy-vibrations pulsing
     through you.
Enjoy the feeling of complete one-ness with all life and all matter.
The glowing radiance is a reflection of your own consciousness.
It is one aspect of your divine nature.
Do not be attached to your old human self.
Do not be alarmed at the new and strange feelings you are having.
If you are attracted now to your old self,
You will be reborn shortly for another round of game-existence.
Exercise humble trust and remain fearless.
You will merge into the heart of the Blessed *Ratnasambhava*,
In a Halo of Rainbow Light,
And attain liberation in the Realm Endowed with Glory.

Instructions for Vision 6: "The Retinal Circus"

O nobly born, listen well:
You are now witnessing the magical dance of forms.
Ecstatic kaleidoscopic patterns explode around you.
All possible shapes come to life before your eyes.
The retinal circus.
The ceaseless play of elements—
Earth, water, air, fire,
In ever-changing forms and manifestations,
Dazzles you with its complexity and variety.
Relax and enjoy the rushing stream.
Do not become attached to any vision or revelation.
Let everything flow through you.
If unpleasant experiences come,
Let them flit by with the rest.
Do not struggle against them.
It all comes from within you.
This is the great lesson in the creativity and power of the brain, freed
    from its learned structures.
Let the cascade of images and associations take you where it will.
Meditate calmly on the knowledge that all these visions are
    emanations of your own consciousness.
This way you can obtain self-knowledge and be liberated.

Instructions for Vision 7: "The Magic Theatre"

O nobly born, listen well:
You are now in the magic theatre of heroes and demons.
Mythical superhuman figures.
Demons, goddesses, celestial warriors, giants,
Angels, Bodhisattvas, dwarfs, crusaders,
Elves, devils, saints, and sorcerers,
Infernal spirits, goblins, knights and emperors.
The Lotus Lord of Dance.
The Wise Old Man. The Divine Child.
The Trickster, The Shapeshifter.
The tamer of monsters.
The mother of gods, the witch.
The moon king. The wanderer.
The whole divine theatre of figures representing the highest reaches
   of human knowledge.
Do not be afraid of them.
They are within you.
Your own creative intellect is the master magician of them all.
Recognize the figures as aspects of your self.
The whole fantastic comedy takes place within you.
Do not become attached to the figures.
Remember the teachings.
You may still attain liberation.

Instructions for the Wrathful Visions

O nobly born, listen carefully:
You were unable to maintain the perfect Clear Light of the First
    Bardo.
Or the serene peaceful visions of the Second.
You are now entering Second Bardo nightmares.
Recognize them.
They are your own thought-forms made visible and audible.
They are products of your own mind with its back to the wall.
They indicate that you are close to liberation.
Do not fear them.
No harm can come to you from these hallucinations.
They are your own thoughts in frightening aspect.
They are old friends.
Welcome them. Merge with them. Join them.
Lose yourself in them.
They are yours.
Whatever you see, no matter how strange and terrifying,
Remember above all that it comes from within you.
Hold onto that knowledge.
As soon as you recognize that, you will obtain liberation.
If you do not recognize them,
Torture and punishment will ensue.
But these too are but the radiances of your own intellect.
They are immaterial.
Voidness cannot injure voidness.
None of the peaceful or wrathful visions,
Blood-drinking demons, machines, monsters, or devils,
Exist in reality
Only within your skull.
This will dissipate your fear. Remember it well.

Third Bardo: Preliminary Instructions

O *(name)*, listen well:
You are now entering the Third Bardo.
Before, while experiencing the peaceful and wrathful visions of the
 Second Bardo,
You could not recognize them.
Through fear you became unconscious.
Now, as you recover,
Your consciousness rises up,
Like a trout leaping forth out of water,
Striving for its original form.
Your former ego has started to operate again.
Do not struggle to figure things out.
If through weakness you are attracted to action and thinking,
You will have to wander amidst the world of game existence,
And suffer pain.
Relax your restless mind.

O *(name)*, you have been unable to recognize the archetypal forms of
 the Second Bardo.
You have thus come down this far.
Now, if you wish to see the truth,
Your mind must rest without distraction.
There is nothing to do,
Nothing to think.
Float back to the unobscured, primordial, bright, void state of your
 intellect.
In this way you will obtain liberation.
If you are unable to relax your mind,
Meditate on *(name of protective figure)*
Meditate on your friends *(name)*
Think of them with profound love and trust,
As overshadowing the crown of your head.
This is of great importance.
Be not distracted.

O *(name)*,
You may now feel the power to perform miraculous feats,
To perceive and communicate with extrasensory power,
To change shape, size and number,
To traverse space and time instantly.
These feelings come to you naturally,
Not through any merit on your part.
Do not desire them.
Do not attempt to exercise them.
Recognize them as signs that you are in the Third Bardo,
In the period of re-entry into the normal world.

O *(name)*,
If you have not understood the above,
At this moment,
As a result of your own mental set,
Frightening visions may come.
Gusts of wind and icy blasts,
Humming and clicking of the controlling machinery,
Mocking laughter.
You may imagine terror producing remarks:
"Guilty," "stupid," "inadequate," "nasty."
Such imagined taunts and paranoid nightmares
Are the residues of selfish, ego-dominated game-playing.
Fear them not.
They are your own mental products.
Remember that you are in the Third Bardo.
You are struggling to re-enter the denser atmosphere of routine game
    existence.
Let this re-entry be smooth and slow.
Do not attempt to use force or will-power.

O *(name)*,
As you are driven here and there by the ever-moving winds of
    karma,
Your mind, having no resting place or focus,
Is like a feather tossed about by the wind,

Or like a rider on the horse or breath,
Ceaselessly and involuntarily you will wander about,
Calling in despair for your old ego.
Your mind races along until you are exhausted and miserable.
Do not hold on to thoughts.
Allow the mind to rest in its unmodified state.
Meditate on the oneness of all energy.
Thus you will be free of sorrow, terror, and confusion.

O *(name)*,
You may feel confused and bewildered.
You may be wondering about your sanity.
You may look at your fellow voyagers and friends,
And sense that they cannot understand you.
You may think; "I am dead! What shall I do?,"
And feel great misery,
Just like a fish cast out of water on red-hot embers.
You may wonder whether you will ever return.
Familiar places, relatives, people known to you appear now as in a
    dream,
Or through a glass darkly.
If you are having such experiences,
Thinking will be of no avail.
Do not struggle to explain.
This is the natural result of your own mental program.
Such feelings indicate that you are in the Third Bardo.
Trust your guide,
Trust your companions,
Trust the Compassionate Buddha,
Meditate calmly and without distraction.

O *(name)*,
You may now feel as if you are being oppressed and squeezed,
Like between rocks and boulders,
Or like inside a cage or prison.
Remember:
These are signs that you are trying to force a return to your ego.

There may be a dull, gray light
Suffusing all objects with a murky glow.
These are all signs of the Third Bardo.
Do not struggle to return.
The re-entry will happen by itself.
Recognize where you are.
Recognition will lead to liberation.

Instructions for Re-entry Visions

O *(name)*,
You have still not understood what is happening.
So far you have been searching for your past personality.
Unable to find it, you may begin to feel that you will never be the
     same again,
That you will come back a changed person.
Saddened by this you will feel self-pity,
You will attempt to find your ego, to regain control.
So thinking, you will wander here and there,
Ceaselessly and distractedly.
Different images of your future self will be seen by you;
The one you are headed for will be seen most clearly.
The special art of these teachings is particularly important at this moment.
Whatever image you see,
Meditate upon it as coming from the Buddha—
That level of existence also exists in the Buddha.
This is an exceedingly profound art.
It will free you from your present confusion.
Meditate upon *(name of protective ideal)* for as long as possible.
Visualize him as a form produced by a magician,
Then let his image melt away,
Starting with the extremities,
Till nothing remains visible.
Put yourself in a state of Clearness and Voidness;
Abide in that state for a while.
Then meditate again on your protective ideal.
Then again on the Clear Light.
Do this alternately.
Afterwards, allow your own mind also to melt away gradually.
Wherever the air pervades, consciousness pervades.
Wherever consciousness pervades, serene ecstasy pervades.
Abide tranquilly in the uncreated state of serenity.
In that state, paranoid rebirth will be prevented.
Perfect enlightenment will be gained.

Instructions for the All-Determining
Influence of Thought

O *(name)*, you may now experience momentary joy,
Followed by momentary sorrow,
Of great intensity,
Like the stretching and relaxing of a catapult.
You will go through sharp mood swings,
All determined by *karma*.
Be not in the least attached to the joys nor displeased by the sorrows.
The actions of your friends or companions may evoke anger or
     shame in you.
If you get angry or depressed,
You will immediately have an experience of hell.
No matter what people are doing,
Make sure that no angry thought can arise.
Meditate upon love for them.
Even at this late stage of the session
You are only one second away from a life-changing joyous discovery.
Remember that each of your companions is Buddha within.
Your mind in its present state having no focus or integrating force,
Being light and continuously moving,
Whatever thought occurs to you,
Positive or negative,
Will wield great power.
You are *extremely* suggestible
Therefore think not of selfish things.
Recall your preparation for the session.
Show pure affection and humble faith.
Through hearing these words,
Recollection will come.
Recollection will be followed by recognition and liberation.

Instructions for Judgment Visions

O *(name)*, if you are experiencing a vision of judgment and guilt,
Listen scarefully:
That you are suffering like this
Is the result of your own mental set.
Your *karma*.
No one is doing anything to you.
There is nothing to do.
Your own mind is creating the problem.
Accordingly float into meditation.
Remember your former beliefs.
Remember the teachings of this manual.
Remember the friendly presence of your companions.
If you do not know how to meditate
Concentrate on any single object or sensation.
Hold this *(hand the wanderer an object)*,
Concentrate on the reality of this,
Recognize the illusory nature of existence and phenomena.
This moment is of great importance.
If you are distracted now it will take you a long time to get out of the
    quagmire of misery.
Up till now the Bardo experiences have come to you and you have
    not recognized them.
You have been distracted.
On this account you have experienced all the fear and terror.
Even though unsuccessful thus far
You may recognize and obtain liberation here.
Your session can still become ecstatic and revelatory.
If you do not know how to meditate, remember *(person's ideal)*.
Remember your companions
Remember this manual.
Think of all these fears and terrifying apparitions as being your own
    ideal,
Or as the compassionate one.

They are divine tests.
Remember your guide.
Repeat the names over and over.
Even though you fall,
You will not be hurt.

Instructions for Sexual Visions

O *(name),*
At this time you may see visions of mating couples.
You are convinced that an orgy is about to take place.
Desire and anticipation seize you,
You wonder what sexual performance is expected of you.
When these visions occur,
Remember to withhold yourself from action or attachment.
Humbly exercise your faith.
Float with the stream.
Trust the process with great fervency.
Meditation and trust in the unity of life are the keys.
If you attempt to enter into your old personality because you are
    attracted or repulsed,
If you try to join the orgy you are hallucinating,
You will be reborn on an animal level.
You will experience possessive desire and jealousy,
You will suffer stupidity and misery.
If you wish to avoid these miseries
Listen and recognize.
Reject the feelings of attraction or repulsion.
Remember the downward pull opposing enlightenment is strong in
    you.
Meditate upon unity with your fellow voyagers.
Abandon jealousy,
Be neither attracted nor repulsed by your sexual hallucinations.
If you are you will wander in misery a long time.
Repeat these words to yourself.
And meditate on them.

Four Methods of Preventing Re-entry

First Method: Meditation on the Buddha

O *(name)*, tranquilly meditate upon your protective figure *(name)*.
He is like the reflecting of the moon in water.
He is apparent yet non-existent.
Like illusion produced by magic.
If you have no special protective figure,
Meditate upon the Buddha or upon me.
With this in mind meditate tranquilly.
Then causing the visualized form of your protective ideal
To melt away from the extremities,
Meditate, without any thought-forming, upon the Void Clear Light.
This is a very profound art.
By virtue of it rebirth is postponed.
A more illuminated future is assured.

Second Method: Meditation on Good Games

(Name), You are now wandering in the Third Bardo.
As a sign of this, look into a mirror and you will not see your usual
    self (show the wanderer a mirror).
At this time you must form a single, firm resolve in your mind.
This is very important.
It is like directing the course of a horse by the use of the reins.
Whatever you desire will come to pass.
Think not of evil actions which might turn the course of your mind.
Remember your spiritual relationship with me,
Or with anyone from whom you have received teaching.
Persevere with good games.
This is essential.
Be not distracted.
Here lies the boundary line between going up or down.
If you give way to indecision for even a second,
You will have to suffer misery for a long, long time,
Trapped in your old habits and games.
This is the moment.
Hold fast to one single purpose.
Remember good games.
Resolve to act according to your highest insight.
This is a time when earnestness and pure love are necessary.
Abandon jealousy.
Meditate upon laughter and trust.
Bear this well at heart.

Third Method: Meditation on Illusion

If still going down and not liberated,
Meditate as follows:
The sexual activities, the manipulation machinery, the mocking
    laughter, dashing sounds and terrifying apparitions,
Indeed all phenomena
Are in their nature, illusions.
However they may appear, in truth they are unreal and fake.
They are like dreams and apparitions,
Non-permanent, non-fixed.
What advantage is there in being attached to them,
Or being afraid of them?
All these are hallucinations of the mind.
The mind itself does not exist,
Therefore why should they?
Only through taking these illusions for real will you wander around
    in this confused existence.
All these are like dreams,
Like echoes,
Like cities of clouds,
Like mirages,
Like mirrored forms,
Like phantasmagoria,
The moon seen in water.
Not real even for a moment.
By holding one-pointedly to that train of thought.
The belief that they are real is dissipated,
And liberation is attained.

Fourth Method: Meditation on the Void

"All substances are part of my own consciousness.
This consciousness is vacuous, unborn, and unceasing."
Thus meditating,
Allow the mind to rest in the uncreated state.
Like the pouring of water into water,
The mind should be allowed its own easy mental posture
In its natural, unmodified condition, clear and vibrant.
By maintaining this relaxed, uncreated state of mind
Rebirth into routine game-reality is sure to be prevented.
Meditate on this until you are certainly free.

Instructions for Choosing the Post-Session Personality

(Name), Listen:
It is almost time to return.
Make the selection of your future personality according to the best
    teaching.
Listen well:
The signs and characteristics of the level of existence to come
Will appear to you in premonitory visions.
Recognize them.
When you find that you have to return to reality,
Try to follow the pleasant delightful visions.
Avoid the dark unpleasant ones.
If you return in panic, a fearful state will follow,
If you strive to escape dark, gloomy scenes, an unhappy state will
    follow,
If you return in radiance, a happy state will follow.
Your mental state now will affect your subsequent level of being.
Whatever you choose,
Choose impartially,
Without attraction or repulsion.
Enter into game-existence with good grace.
Voluntarily and freely.
Remain calm.
Remember the teachings.